BRITAIN'S LOST MINES

THE VANISHED KINGDOM OF THE MEN
WHO CARVED OUT THE NATION'S WEALTH

BRITAIN'S LOST MINES

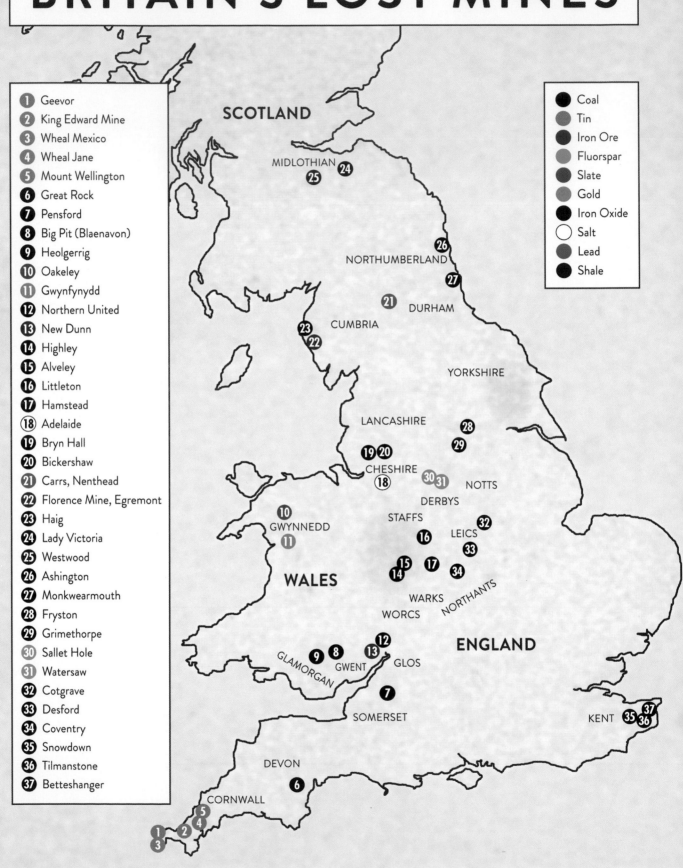

1 Geevor
2 King Edward Mine
3 Wheal Mexico
4 Wheal Jane
5 Mount Wellington
6 Great Rock
7 Pensford
8 Big Pit (Blaenavon)
9 Heolgerrig
10 Oakeley
11 Gwynfynydd
12 Northern United
13 New Dunn
14 Highley
15 Alveley
16 Littleton
17 Hamstead
18 Adelaide
19 Bryn Hall
20 Bickershaw
21 Carrs, Nenthead
22 Florence Mine, Egremont
23 Haig
24 Lady Victoria
25 Westwood
26 Ashington
27 Monkwearmouth
28 Fryston
29 Grimethorpe
30 Sallet Hole
31 Watersaw
32 Cotgrave
33 Desford
34 Coventry
35 Snowdown
36 Tilmanstone
37 Betteshanger

Coal
Tin
Iron Ore
Fluorspar
Slate
Gold
Iron Oxide
Salt
Lead
Shale

SCOTLAND

MIDLOTHIAN

NORTHUMBERLAND

DURHAM

CUMBRIA

YORKSHIRE

LANCASHIRE

CHESHIRE

NOTTS

DERBYS

STAFFS

LEICS

GWYNNEDD

WALES

WARKS

NORTHANTS

WORCS

ENGLAND

GLAMORGAN

GWENT

GLOS

SOMERSET

KENT

DEVON

CORNWALL

BRITAIN'S LOST MINES

THE VANISHED KINGDOM OF THE MEN
WHO CARVED OUT THE NATION'S WEALTH

CHRIS ARNOT

To the men who risked limbs, lungs, and sometimes their lives, to extract the basic materials that made our own lives worth living.

ACKNOWLEDGEMENTS

Many thanks to those who have shared their mining memories and anecdotes. Apologies to anyone inadvertently omitted from the lengthy list below, which is in no particular order.

Chris Lilburn, Sean Farrell, Chris Stewart, Luke Unsworth, Bill Scriven, George Poyner, David Poyner, Linda Hirseman, Eddie Hirseman, Marcus Hitchens, Graham Walford, Dennis Bache, Stan Jones, Tony Brooks, Peter Savage, Dennis Way, Alan Taylor, Richard Freeborn, Mike Bacon, Frank Forster, Tony Ward, Reg Hackett, Leslie Brownhill, Bob le Marchant, Arthur Ball, Rob Bailey, Francis Hillier and Bill Morris of the Somerset District Miners' Welfare Trust, Nick Turner, George Archibald, Tom Young and Ellie Swinbank of the Scottish Mining Museum, Richard McBrearty of the Scottish Football Museum, Rob Ridley, Richard Ellis, Harry Malkin, Brian Lewis, Steve Lane, Dave Harvey, John Belcher, Ray Wright, Jonathan Wright, Elaine Mormon, Dennis Gething, George Hall, Dr Peter Claughton of the National Association of Mining History Organisations, Nick Booker, Larry Routledge, Margaret Routledge, Mike Kirkup, Deborah Moffat of the Woodhorn Mining Museum, the Durham Mining Museum, Davey Hopper of the Durham Miners' Association, Chris Hall of the Wearmouth Colliery Social Welfare Club, John Humphreys, Tom Roughead, Dr Dafydd Roberts of the National Slate Museum, Wales, Jim Davies, Keith and Colin Owen, Jason Rose of the Aylesham Skills Factory, Coalfields Heritage Initiative, Kent, Peter Jackson, Gilbert Finlinson, Gary Connell, Pamela Telford, Tom Norman, Mick Botterill, Tom Hughes, Kelvin Green, Mog Stevenson, Graham Burrows, Tony and Jim Cairns, Harry Minton, Russell Wuffendin, Alan Davies, Norman Prior, George Harris, Mike Astill, Alan Parry, Ron Murphy, Michael Gladwin, Mick Chewings, Gerry Hopper, Danny Gillespie, Elsie Smith, Cllr Steve Houghton of Barnsley Council, Robert Haines, Elwyn Marshall, Ceri Thompson, John Perritt, Russell Waite, Andrew Furlong, Mick Goddard and Barrie Sutton.

Thanks, too, to Graham Coster, Robin Harvie and Melissa Smith of Aurum for their encouragement. To Lucy Warburton for finding so many magnificent pictures, and to Chris Shamwana and Madison Clare at Ghost for the beautiful design.

First published 2013 by
Aurum Press Limited
74-77 White Lion Street
London N1 9PF
www.aurumpress.co.uk

Text copyright © Chris Arnot 2013

A catalogue record for this book is available from the British Library.

ISBN 978 1 78131 070 0

10 9 8 7 6 5 4 3 2 1
2017 2016 2015 2014 2013

Designed by Ghost
Map designed by timpeters.co.uk
Printed in China

CONTENTS

INTRODUCTION

TWENTY MINUTES FROM the Regency elegance of Bath and half an hour from the Glastonbury Festival, you might drive through the Somerset village of Paulton and notice what appears to be a dormant volcano looming over the landscape. It's known locally as 'The Batch' and is really a colliery spoil tip. Apart from the commemorative headstocks outside the mining museum in nearby Radstock, it's one of the few reminders that until the 1970s men worked under the green fields of southwest England in some of the worst conditions known in the British coalfield. Youths were still being used as human pit ponies, tethered by chains and hooked on to carts of coal to be dragged from low and dusty seams, until the mid-twentieth century.

Until the second half of the 1980s, meanwhile, almost naked men of Kent were toiling nearly 3,000 feet beneath the 'Garden of England' in such heat that sweat had to be poured out of their boots at regular intervals. The letter-writers of Tunbridge Wells would have been disgusted had they been aware of the existence of Snowdown Colliery, otherwise known as The Inferno. Same county, different planet. The miners of Snowdown, as well as nearby Tilmanstone and Betteshanger, were toiling only fifteen minutes' drive from Canterbury Cathedral and half an hour from the fashionable beach huts of Whitstable. Yet those men and their families were isolated from the rest of the county, hidden away on estates as different from the average Kentish town and village as it's possible to imagine. How many visitors to Deal, for instance, are aware of the Mill Hill estate on the edge of town, built to house the mining families of Betteshanger?

Elsewhere in the UK there is far more imprint on the landscape of mining's lengthy legacy, as this book shows with a wealth of evocative visual imagery. All along the jagged north Cornish coast, from Pendeen to Land's End, the chimneys of crumbling tin-mine engine houses still stand as gaunt reminders that this was once the most intensely mined part of the country. Huge heaps of slate encircle the North Wales town of Blaenau Ffestiniog where it sometimes looks as though the mountains have been turned inside out. Nobody would be surprised to learn that some of those 'mountains' in the steep, greened-over valleys of South Wales are man-made. But it's also true of some of the sculpted hills flanking the wide brown river that flows through Shropshire's beautiful Severn Valley.

Other stunning parts of the country, including the Lake District and the Forest of Dean, counted a substantial mining community among their residents. In the not too distant past, indeed, much of Britain was being mined for all manner of minerals and ores, from the far southeast of England to the west of Scotland and beyond.

Today that seems almost inconceivable. Mining disasters are terrible events that happen in faraway countries of which we know little – in South America, South Africa or the former Soviet Union rather than in South Wales, South Yorkshire or Lancashire. On either side of the Pennines, meanwhile, the pit-head baths of once-thriving collieries are buried under retail parks. It's yet another illustration of how the world's first

Top: Pickets clashing with police at Orgreave Coking Plant, 1984.

Bottom: Some mines have reopened but, like the Llechwedd Slate Caverns in North Wales, only as tourist attractions.

industrial nation now relies on shopping to employ much of its workforce.

This book is an exploration of a mining tradition that goes back, in parts, to Roman times. Sometimes it has left huge scars on the landscape as well as on the men who inhaled lungfuls of dust daily. Sometimes it has disappeared without trace. With it has gone a unique culture that spawned brass bands and male voice choirs, terrifying fast bowlers, brilliant footballers and (mainly Scottish) managers. Not to mention rock-hard rugby players – league in the north of England and union in the south of Wales.

While cleaning up mining's black-dusted footprints, it's important that we don't throw out the memories with the dirty water. Within another generation, many of the men who worked underground will no longer be with us. We should listen to their stories while we can.

Although I belatedly discovered that my paternal grandfather had been a miner, I have no first-hand experience of an occupation which perhaps only a masochist or an enthusiast who has rarely had to do it day in, day out could describe as pleasurable. Many of those who had little alternative but to pit themselves against an alien underworld to earn a living are remarkable men. Meeting so many of them has been a privilege. So too, incidentally, has meeting those devotees who seem to like nothing better than being bent almost double in confined spaces with dirty water dripping down the back of their necks.

Water was an ongoing intruder into our mines, always seeping through thick layers of earth and rock. I found myself up to my knees in the stuff after following an enthusiastic geologist into what had been Devon's last metal mine. With the help of WD-40, he had managed to prise open the gates for the first time since they slammed shut in 1969. A few months later, on a freezing day near the highest market town in England, my just-about-dry boots tentatively followed another geologist into a disused Cumbrian lead mine. Every now and then I felt a sensation that had become familiar on my visits to an old Cornish tin mine and a former Welsh coal mine – the crack of cranium on overhead rock. Luckily in all cases, the cranium was protected by a helmet with a much-needed light on the front.

On these occasions I did my best to disguise the relief that I felt on emerging into fresh air. It's difficult to imagine what it must have been like to spend hour after hour, day after day in there, blasting and drilling, swinging picks and shovels, sometimes in unforgiving heat and dust, while encumbered by those weighty pieces of equipment necessary for survival.

At various times in British history, depending on the market, miners have been hired to truffle out minerals on behalf of wealthy individuals or companies that had the wherewithal to pay their wages and still make enough to offer a decent return to their shareholders and not insubstantial profits to themselves. Very occasionally one or two closed mines reopen as new uses emerge for old minerals, as is the case with fluorspar mining in Derbyshire, or new methods provide more accurate ways of locating precious veins buried in layers of rock, as would appear to be the case with gold mining in Scotland.

Here you will find the stories of a former gold mine in an enchanted part of Wales; of tin mines and iron ore mines as well as lead mines, slate mines, a shale-oil mine, fluorspar mines and even a couple of salt mines in unlikely parts of England. There are thirty chapters, but each one covers far more than the mine mentioned in the heading. It's no use trying to tell even some of the story of mining in South Wales or South Yorkshire, for instance, by focusing on just one mine.

The bulk of the stories brought to the surface here are from men who dug coal, as their fathers did before them. I make no apologies for that. This island rests on coal. Coal powered the Industrial Revolution and the railway system that carried its products. Coal was the main source of heat and light for our homes until comparatively recently. The men who dug it out, usually at some risk to their health and wellbeing, didn't do it out of the kindness of their hearts. Of course they didn't. They did it because they needed to support their families and there were few alternative means of doing so for those who were born into mining communities. But the rest of us were the sometimes ungracious beneficiaries of their labour.

'It is only because miners sweat their guts out that superior persons can remain superior,' George Orwell wrote in the stirring final paragraph of his memorable first-hand account of coal mining in *The Road to Wigan Pier*. You can read the paragraph in full in the section on Bryn Hall, the colliery that the great man visited in 1936. Were he writing today, he would have to put that paragraph in the past tense because we no longer rely on coal for light and heat – and that coal we do use is mainly shipped in from distant parts of the globe.

Stephen Armstrong, author of *The Road to Wigan*

Pier Revisited, published in 2011, is quite revealing on how this state of affairs came about. On page fifty-eight he writes: 'From the 1950s and 1960s there are Hansard debates and secret documents in the Cabinet archive discussing the closure of pit towns and the coalfields – all with a political subtext: the miners were essential but troublesome.' And in 1974 (shortly after Edward Heath had called and lost a snap election against the background of a strike by the National Union of Mineworkers) *The Economist* published a leaked document called the Ridley Report.

'Drawn up by Nicholas Ridley MP, founding member of the free-market cadre the Selsdon Group, it explained how the next Conservative government should take on the NUM,' Armstrong goes on.

Ten years later Ridley was a member of the Thatcher Government which implemented that policy. Now you can argue that the NUM leadership walked straight into the trap; that NUM leader Arthur Scargill should have called a ballot; that his demands were unrealistic and that desperation was no excuse for the behaviour of some of his more thuggish supporters. You can also argue that emissions from coal-fired power stations were bad for the environment – although protecting the planet doesn't appear to have been high on the government's agenda at the time. The fact remains that at the height of the strike in 1984, North Sea oil revenues peaked at twelve billion pounds. Had we invested a fraction of that money in modern techniques and cleaner coal – as happened in, for instance, Germany – we might still have a manufacturing base, Armstrong argues. 'So we had the money but we spent it. On fuelling tax cuts and temporary booms.'

The largest of Britain's few remaining collieries, Daw Mill in Warwickshire, closed in March 2013 after a devastating fire underground. Over 650 men were made redundant, an all too familiar story. Maltby Colliery in South Yorkshire ceased working the following month, a few days before the somewhat more widely publicised death of Lady Thatcher. This time 540 or so jobs were lost. Mining was a labour-intensive industry and the sheer numbers involved mean that more British families than you might think have members who worked underground a generation or two ago.

The destruction of our domestic coal industry ensured that millions of untapped tons remain buried forever. It also buried a way of life. Ask any former miner what he misses and the response is always the same. Some will call it 'comradeship', others 'camaraderie'. They didn't just work together, they played and sang together in bands and choirs. They competed against each other when it came to racing pigeons or growing enormous vegetables, but they played in the same football and cricket teams. And they drank together after work or play, too much in some cases. Punch-ups outside miners' welfares and pit-village pubs were not exactly uncommon. But once underground, miners were brothers under the dust-encrusted skin, looking out for each other's wellbeing in what was an unpredictable and dangerous environment.

Coal mining communities were torn apart by the events of 1984–5. Most have never recovered, despite investment by subsequent governments and indeed the European Union. Some animosities have healed with time, others have festered. But although the subject is unavoidable, this book is not really about the strike and its aftermath. It's largely about what went on before, in collieries and in other mines.

There may not be as many complex geological details here as some readers would like. But thanks anyway to the enthusiasts who opened my eyes to what went on underground. Above all, thanks to the many former miners who have showed me the sites of their old workplaces and shared with me their memories, some touching, some sad, some funny, all enlightening. There are, of course, museums and oral archives where miners' voices are recorded for posterity. But the stories here are not just from one mine, not just from one county, not just from one coalfield. They're from all over mainland Britain and it seems to me that they're worth preserving between hard covers to help ensure that they too are in no danger of being buried forever.

Bickershaw Colliery with Pennington flash in the foreground, near Wigan, c.1930s.

Cornish tin miners making
the most of the sea air.

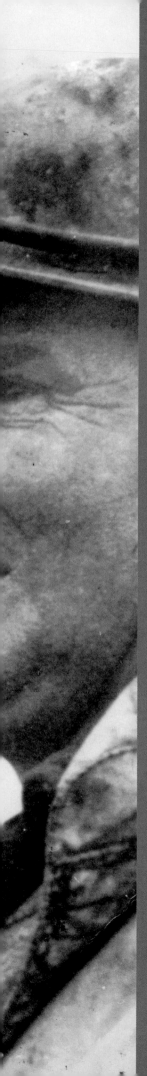

GEEVOR AND KING EDWARD

ONCE THE SEA FRET has lifted, the first thing you take in are the chimneys. They seem to stretch all the way along the rugged coastline from here at the former Geevor mine in Pendeen to St Just, some seven miles away, and then on towards Land's End. Along with the crumbling granite engine houses beneath them, they are the most prominent and poignant reminders that Cornwall was once more intensively mined than any other area of Britain.

This part, towards the western tip of the county and indeed the country, was known as Cape Cornwall. It accommodated a major concentration of metal mines. Perhaps the most famous of them all was Botallack, which extended 400 metres out under the Atlantic Ocean. Apart from tin, it gave its name to a secondary copper mineral that became known as Botallackite.

Cornish copper mining peaked in the 1860s and was all but at an end by 1880. Tin mining continued despite growing competition from elsewhere in the world, notably Malaya, during the 1880s and 90s. It boomed briefly in Cornwall before the First World War, only to face a slump soon after. From then on, upturns in the price of tin led to sporadic revivals, but comparatively few mines would survive into the late twentieth century.

Geevor was one of them. In fact it stayed open until 1990, and is now part of a World Heritage Site providing fascinating insights into an industry that has drilled itself deeply into Cornish identity. But before concentrating on Geevor, let's briefly nip back up what is now the A30 to Camborne, the core of another spread of former metal mines. At one time or another there have been some 300 between Camborne and Truro, just over thirteen miles away. Looking out from one of the Grade II listed buildings at the former King Edward mine, more of those haunting chimneys seem to stretch all the way down the valley as far as the eye can see. The best-known was Dolcoath, once the deepest and most productive mine in all Cornwall. Eventually it reached a depth of 1,000m (over 3,000 feet). Men employed on the lower levels needed two to three hours to go down and return to the surface.

By 1920 Dolcoath was practically worked out and, after another collapse in the price of tin, the decision was taken to close it down. King Edward went the following year. It was a much smaller operation, but it did house the Camborne School of Mines, founded in 1888 and now part of the University of Exeter's Cornwall Campus at Penryn.

Tony Brooks is a graduate of the school and chairman of the not-for-profit company that manages King Edward as another part of the World Heritage Site. He is also well placed to talk about Cornish migration, having worked for eleven years at a copper mine in Zambia, eventually becoming senior underground manager. Leaving

Cornwall to look for mining work elsewhere in the world is part of a lengthy tradition. Between 1815 and 1915, it's estimated that some 250,000 people left the county and moved abroad. Many came back eventually. By all accounts, there are still plenty of folk in Camborne and elsewhere who will tell you that they've never been to London or even Land's End, but they have been to America.

'They'll also tell you that they've got a grandfather in Ballarat [Australia] and an uncle in Grass Valley, California,' says Tony. 'I was in Grass Valley the year before last, walked up the main street and found Cornish pasties on sale. There was the Cornish flag flying outside a hotel. At one time, seventy per cent of the miners there were Cornish. Emigration continued right up to recent times. When mines closed here, they had to look elsewhere.'

Certainly there were precious few jobs elsewhere in Cornwall. Admittedly Holman Brothers of Camborne employed quite a few in their heyday, although that was rather a long time ago. The company made mining equipment and somehow survived until 2001. No wonder Cornwall is so dependent on tourism. Those of us who visit for holidays may note the number of second-home owners and the profusion of fancy restaurants inspired by Rick Stein and Jamie Oliver. But we tend to forget that incomes among the indigenous population make this one of the poorest parts of the UK.

Above: Walking home at the end of the shift.

Opposite top: Asket and gang.

Opposite below: The Queen opens the sub-incline extension, 28 November 1980.

At least Tony was able to get a job as an academic at the School of Mines when he returned from Zambia. Apart from knowing a lot about managing mines, he has some experience of what you might call the metal-face. As a student, he worked briefly at the Great Rock mine in Devon, looking for the iron oxide used in rust-resisting paints (see page 27). He also had a spell at Geevor.

'I was there for a month in 1962 when I'd just left school and was waiting to join the School of Mines,' he explains. 'I was eighteen and I remember it being incredibly hard work. A lot of water kept percolating through the rock, and it had to be pumped out. And at the deeper levels it became really quite hot. You were drilling into hard, almost vertical rock.' So was it dusty? 'By that time they'd cut right back on the incidence of silicosis by putting jets of water in the drills. So, no, it wasn't too dusty, but it was very noisy, like being in a confined space with a motorbike. There were a lot of deaf miners until they introduced ear protectors.'

He describes the extraction of tin from the surrounding granite as 'like taking the jam filling out of a sponge cake and trying to leave the sponge behind'. Veins of tin, known as lodes, were blasted and drilled from the rock but, inevitably, a lot of rock came with them. Back in the eighteenth and nineteenth centuries, the waste had to be chipped off with chisels and hammers by burly women known as bal-maidens. The coming of electricity, however, brought with it crushing and stamping machines. Not to mention 'shaking tables' from which tin filings were finally sifted from crushed and finely ground rock.

That month at Geevor convinced Tony of one thing: 'It would pay me to study so that I didn't have to do mining at the bottom end for the rest of my life.' But for the vast majority of miners, higher education was not an option they felt equipped to consider. Dennis Way started at Geevor when he was twenty-five in 1971, first as a general labourer and then as a 'stoper'. In other words, he was responsible for extracting the minerals from the lode. 'You always worked in pairs,' he says. 'You had to be on the same wavelength and be a little bit hungry. There was good money to be made here in the seventies.' Between thirty and fifty pounds on occasions – a *day*, that is. This was at a time when many working men earned less than thirty quid a week. But then most working men weren't drilling through solid rock and using gelignite as a tool of the trade.

'What you did was drill the holes you needed for a tunnel or "drive" as we termed it,' Dennis goes on. 'You'd put in thirty-two holes, say, to a depth of eight feet. Towards the end of your working day [around 2.30 p.m.] you'd start charging them with gelignite. Then you linked up the circuit, connected it to your main cable and walked back two hundred yards before hitting it with the blaster. You went back in the morning at seven a.m. sharp and, hopefully, you'd have about ten tons of rock. You'd have to clean it up a bit, put it in the wagons and take it back to the shaft bottom. Then you'd start drilling again.'

Dennis's partner was Ian Davey, known to one and all as 'Bomber'. His nickname was earned during his time as a 'grizzly man' – a 'grizzly' being a grid of iron bars that allowed ore of the correct size to travel to the bottom of a mine shaft, ready to be hoisted to the surface. The conventional way of breaking up the rock to pass through the bars was to set about it with a sledgehammer. Alternatively you could use explosives, and 'Bomber' used more than most, blasting up to fifteen or more lumps of rock in one big bang. Those ear protectors were not just for the noise of drilling.

Bomber Davey is no longer with us, and it's obvious that Dennis misses not just him but all his mates from the mine. In that respect he's no different from any miner anywhere in the UK. They all miss the 'camaraderie' of men who shared a hard and dirty job in confined quarters and the bleak humour that went with it. 'We earned good money and we socialised a lot together,' he recalls. 'The village boomed for a while.' Not just the pubs and the shops either. The mine depended on electricians, masons, carpenters and other local traders.

Today Pendeen appears to be largely dependent on summer visitors. There are a couple of pubs doing bed and breakfast, a chip shop, a pottery shop, a jewellery shop and a Costcutter store. When I ask Dennis whether they were conscious of holidaymakers sunning themselves on nearby beaches while he and his mates were drilling rock underground, he shrugs and says, 'Don't forget you were up at the surface just after three. Then you could go to the beach or go fishing. That's how a lot of miners supplemented their income in the early days.'

By the early 1980s there was no need. Wages were high and Geevor was employing 400 men. It was also looking to expand under the sea, having taken over the nearby Levant mine. What the men didn't realise at the time was that the price of tin was being kept artificially high by the futures markets. A crash was inevitable. It came in 1985 when the International Tin Agreement came to an end and the price collapsed. 'I left the following year and became a postman,' says Dennis. It must have been pleasant to be out in the open air, I suggest. 'Yeah, but it wasn't anywhere near the same money.' He's now a guide at his former place of work.

Geevor closed in 1990 by which time the workforce was half what it had been a decade earlier. 'One of the many reasons why there's no mining in Cornwall today is that they can scoop it up in places like China and Indonesia, and they can dredge it out of rivers in Malaysia.' Dennis is obviously sceptical about rumours that the price of tin – rising again on the back of a European ruling on the need for lead-free solder in electronics and plumbing – will lead to a Cornish mining revival. Exploratory work is going on at the South Crofty mine, between Camborne and Redruth, which was the last to close in 1998. It may yet be the first to reopen. We shall see.

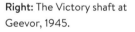

Left: Group of students and miners at Engine Shaft, King Edward, c.1903.

In the next chapter, we're going to follow Dennis into a mine that closed long before Geevor opened in 1911. Before we don our hard hats, however, it's time to have a quick look inside the showers where Geevor men scrubbed themselves clean after a hard day's work. Our guide is Peter Savage, deputy manager at the Geevor Tin Mine museum who has already showed me the mill where the rock was crushed and ground into sand for the tin to be sifted out. There were other by-products as well. Iron sulphides were sold to a smelter in Finland. Arsenic is still used in the glass industry as well as in the infra-red light-emitting diode in your TV's remote control. So what happened to the remains of the sand when the tin and other minerals had been extracted? 'Some was sold to local gravel companies and the rest was shoved off the cliffs,' says Peter. 'I used to be a train driver and, when I looked out to sea, I always knew it was a weekend because the water below those cliffs would be blue rather than red.'

The men used to wash off that red dust with green soap. Those of us of a certain age will remember our mothers keeping a huge oblong bar of it on the side of the kitchen sink. They used it for scrubbing collars or floors or sometimes grubby knees. The aroma was not appealing. 'You could still smell it,' Pete confides, 'when we moved in here ten years after the mine closed and set about recreating the outbuildings as they would have been around the mid-1980s.'

And you can obviously smell it now because there are bars of the stuff resting on the rim of chipped white tiles. Nearby is 'the dry', the miners' word for the lockers where they hung their clean clothes and, separately, their working clothes. Here are red-stained jackets and plastic macs (remember all that water). And here's an unsavoury-looking Thermos and a T-shirt full of holes with the words 'Alright my luvver?' just about discernible through the dust. The towels hanging on functional hooks are as thin and rough as sandpaper. They wouldn't pass muster in any of the local B&Bs.

All that's missing is the noise – the rowdy, bawdy banter of men who've finished work for the day. A contributor to the visitors' book has summed it up well in three words that could apply to Geevor in particular or Cornish mining in general:

'Feel the silence.'

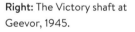

Right: The Victory shaft at Geevor, 1945.

WHEAL MEXICO

A GROUP OF BIKERS are just arriving as I make my way out to the car park. 'Don't bother taking off your helmets, lads,' I shout across to them. But they simply look baffled – perhaps because they haven't taken their helmets off yet and can't hear what I'm saying. Whether they do or not matters little, come to think of it. Yellow hard hats are available and I'd advise anybody over 4 feet tall to put one on and keep it on if you venture inside Wheal Mexico, which used to be a mine a long time ago.

A very long time ago, as it happens. It was being mined in the late eighteenth or early nineteenth century, though it's difficult to pinpoint the exact dates because no original plans exist for such shallow workings. Certainly it was never in the pantheon of important Cornish metal mines. The only reason we're inside it is because it's comparatively dry and we're allowed in, under supervision. Other – much bigger and deeper – mines here on the coastline from Pendeen to St Just and beyond are completely flooded.

Wheal Mexico was only rediscovered in 1995. It's not much more than a series of interconnected 'adits', as they call tunnels down here, built into the cliff rather than a couple of thousand feet or so below it. The great advantage for visitors to the nearby Geevor mining museum is that they can be shown around the sort of rock face that Cornish miners would have worked without having to climb into a lift shaft and be plunged into the bowels of the earth. But don't run away with the idea that this is a comfortable stroll through a rocky grotto similar to Cheddar Gorge.

'Mind your head,' says my guide, former Geevor miner Dennis Way, for the umpteenth time. Crack. Once again I've stood up slightly too early or not bent down soon enough to avoid a piece of overhanging rock. Were it not for this helmet I would have a gash in my head like the slit in a piggy bank. Luckily, there are parts of the mine where a man of just under 6 feet can stand up and look around.

'This is a lode,' Dennis is saying, pointing to a slightly darker vein of red rock running through this jagged granite. 'It's mainly iron oxide, but you'll find tin in there as well as lead, copper, zinc and arsenic.' The lode is quite high up from the ground, I point out. 'They'd have had a ladder or a small platform,' Dennis assures me. 'We don't know how many men worked here. Maybe ten, maybe fewer. And in those days there would have been boys as well, from the ages of nine or ten.'

At least they would have been able to get to the lodes without having to bend double, I'm thinking as Dennis reflects: 'These people would have worked all hours using hammers and chisels.' No electric drills in those days. No gelignite either. 'They could have been using gunpowder by the 1700s,' he points out.

One of the main differences with coal mining is that the rock here is much harder and it tends to be vertical, or at least 70 to 80 degrees to the ground. Another difference is the lack of gas – the sort of gas that causes explosions, anyway. 'The only gas prevalent in Cornish mines was radon, emitted from granite and harmful in the long

term,' says Dennis. Colourless and odourless, radon gives off radiation.

The mines here were also plagued by water in abundance. Cornwall is a wet county and rain percolates downward. Here in Wheal Mexico, just above sea level, I can feel it dripping through the rock and landing on my helmet with a plop. During the early part of the Industrial Revolution, the steam engine was used extensively in Cornish mines to enable men to drill without being up to their waists or even their necks. The inventor James Watt and his business partner Matthew Boulton made the long journey from Birmingham to west Cornwall at frequent intervals. They charged mine owners a royalty for the privilege of using their machines.

By the early 1800s, Cornwall's own Richard Trevithick had evolved the steam engine into a beam engine, using higher pressure and creating the possibility of pumping out water at a faster rate. Not surprisingly, it became known as the 'Cornish engine' and was improved first by William Sims and then by Samuel Grose after Trevithick left for South America in 1816.

For the next eleven years he travelled from Peru to Ecuador, then to Colombia and Costa Rica. Not to Mexico, though, as far as we know. Wheal Mexico, it seems, was one of several Cornish mines with a Mexican tag, as it was thought that Mexico's wealth from silver would be a good omen for investors in tin.

A 'wheal', incidentally, is a Cornish word for a mine

The chimneys that stretch all along the rugged coastline from Pendine to St Just and beyond.

or working. And while we're on the subject of dialect, I ask Dennis what the Cornish word is for what coal miners call 'snap'.

'Mossel,' he says. 'It's short for "morsel". You tried to find a dry part of the mine where you could have a sandwich and a flask of tea, or maybe a pasty. I used to take a home-made pasty to work sometimes. Trouble is, you had to eat it cold.'

As we emerge from Wheal Mexico, I stretch my back and a drop of water slides off the peak of my helmet and splashes on to my notebook. The protective coat I've been given is covered in patches of red from where I've brushed against the rock.

It's mid-morning and the sea fret has long gone.

Blinking in the sunshine, I gaze across at the gaunt outline of the former Levant Mine. It jutted some distance out under the Atlantic and I try to imagine what it would have been like to come back up to sea level after nearly eight hours underneath it. Your muscles would be aching and your ears ringing. You'd be soaked in sweat and your eyes would be adjusting to the light. Did those men have the time or inclination to take in the view along this stunning coastline?

Some would, perhaps; some wouldn't. Maybe they took it for granted. They'd be more concerned to get in that shower for an astringent rub down with green household soap and a rough towel before climbing into clean clothes and heading home. One thing's for sure: whatever those miners were paid, they earned every penny.

WHEAL JANE AND MOUNT WELLINGTON

FROM ALAN TAYLOR'S FRONT WINDOW we can see the hills rising above Truro Station. Paddington is just five hours away. But to most former Cornish tin miners, some of whom have travelled halfway across the globe in search of work, London remains as remote and otherworldly as the dark side of the moon. Alan is an exception. When the Wheal Jane mine closed twenty-two years ago, there were no jobs for a man of his experience in Cornwall (surprise, surprise). So he became health and safety consultant to the London Borough of Barnet.

Aged fifty-six at the time, he took with him an impressive qualification. 'I'd done the equivalent job at Wheal Jane since 1984 and nobody had died. Before I took over, the mine had averaged one fatality a year. It may have been just luck,' he muses. More likely he had brought to the job the experience of a poacher turned gamekeeper.

'My predecessor had no experience of mining,' he confides. Alan, on the other hand, had been at it since the mid-1960s when he was made redundant from Holman's of Camborne, manufacturers of mining equipment. 'The problem with contract mining was that you had to drill and blast a lot of rock to get paid and that, in turn, was the biggest problem with health and safety. I knew that men would cut corners because I'd done it myself.'

He had worked at Geevor and many fathoms under the Atlantic at Levant. 'There was one dry place to have a mossel break [the Cornish term for lunch] and the same conversation would come up every day: what would you do if the sea broke in?' Alan pauses and shakes his head. 'There would have been nowhere to escape to, of course. If I knew then what I know now, they'd have had to pay me even more to work there.'

And how much did they pay you?

'Well, my best pay packet was in 1971 or '2 when I'd been working at Wheal Jane for two or three years and came out with £450 for a fortnight.'

You don't have to be a mathematical genius to work out that that's £225 a week – almost ten times what I was earning at the time as a trainee journalist on a magazine in the West End of London. Mind you, Alan and his mates were working considerably harder than I was in conditions that I wouldn't even have wished on my bone-idle editor, a man who tended to spend a couple of hours at his desk before departing for his Soho club at 12.30 and returning around 4 p.m.

'And don't forget,' Alan adds, 'there were plenty of times when you didn't earn good money from mining. After my first fortnight at Geevor, I ended up owing the

Mount Wellington tin mine
cresting the horizon.

company twenty quid.'

Wheal Jane was slightly inland from Geevor, but still in the west of the county, between the villages of Baldhu and Chacewater. It was considered to be a modern mine. Although it had had previous lives in the eighteenth, nineteenth and early twentieth centuries, it's reopening in 1969 after a gap of twenty-three years was something of a revelation to miners who had come to work there from elsewhere. Much development work had been done underground and on improving processing facilities above ground.

'There was a big shaft,' Alan recalls, 'which meant there was access for big machines such as scoop trams. They were like front-loaded road diggers that could pick up three tons of rock at a time. And the lodes were much wider than at other mines in the area.'

Easier to separate the tin and other metal from the surrounding rock then?

'Oh yes, once the mine owners, Consolidated Goldfields, had come up with the right process.'

I suggest it must have been a bit of a doddle compared to Geevor and Levant.

'Oh, no. You still had to work as hard as you could to make as much money as you could.'

While you could, he might have added. Another problem with being a miner was that you never knew when your living was going to be taken away from you. That was particularly so in Cornwall where your chances of employment depended on the price of tin on the international market. Wheal Jane closed again in 1978 when the price dropped and Consolidated Gold pulled out. So, too, did the Canadian company that was running the neighbouring mine at Mount Wellington, just across the Bissoe Valley. It, too, was closed for the time being.

Top: Untreated water flooding into the River Carnon and onward into the estuary.

Middle: Wheal Jane as it was in 1980.

Bottom: The new environmentally friendly site of Wheal Jane.

Both mines were exceptionally leaky and, if one stopped pumping, then both would flood. Alan remembers taking part in a march to lobby Parliament that saw some tin miners venturing to Planet London for the first and last time. 'With the help of a few helpful local MPs, particularly the late David Penhaligon, the government was persuaded to keep the pumps going until a new owner could be found,' he says.

Enter Robert L. Sprinkel III, an American entrepreneur who had made and lost several fortunes by going around the world, reopening mines and then selling them on – in this case to Carnon Consolidated, a subsidiary of Rio Tinto Zinc, the company once described by Conservative Prime Minister Edward Heath as 'the unacceptable face of capitalism'. Somehow Wheal Jane survived the collapse of the International Tin Agreement in 1985 and limped on until 1991, whereupon the long-threatened deluge became imminent.

'We used to pump out four million gallons of water a day,' says Mike Bacon, chief engineer from 1986 until just before the closure. Mount Wellington was even wetter. During the 1970s, the proportion of water being pumped out to ore being brought up was forty to one – an all-time world record. The water at Wheal Jane, however, was particularly acidic. 'It was to do with geology,' says Mike. 'As it percolated down through the rock, it picked up a lot of acid content from the copper sulphate, iron oxide and arsenic. I'd taken voluntary redundancy shortly before both mines closed, but I had a good idea what would happen if they turned off the pumps.'

What happened was an environmental disaster. On 4 January 1992, stormy conditions forced pumping to stop and 320 million litres of untreated water burst from the confines of the mine. Much of it found its way into the nearby River Carnon and flowed onward into the estuary, killing fish and contaminating bird life. In the absence of any modern-day Moses to perform miracles on the 'red sea', it fell to the Environment Agency to sort out the mess. By 2002, ten years after the toxic flood, water treatment costs were put at £20 million.

Over ten years on again and you can still see the settlement tanks set up at the time to stop more polluted water running into the sea. Nearby is the weighbridge for the former mine. The wheel from the top of the shaft has been retained as the gateway to what is now the Wheal Jane group of companies, many of them involved in mining equipment, mineral testing and consultancy work on a global basis. A solar panels company now occupies the site of the main former mining buildings.

Renewable energy sources are much in evidence right across this valley where the steam engines of the Industrial Revolution had thundered away below ground over two centuries previously. All sorts of initiatives using wind, solar and geo-thermal power are under way on the sprawling site of the former Mount Wellington mine.

Since 2007 it has been owned by Richard Freeborn from Kensa Engineering Ltd, manufacturers of ground source heat pumps. Not that he can take an active role in that or any of the other companies on this site. There would be a conflict with his other current role as – wait for it – team technical adviser on renewable heat incentives for the Department of Energy and Climate Change. Once a fortnight he boards the night sleeper from Truro to Paddington, presumably changing into his Whitehall attire en route.

Today, though, it's high summer and he's dressed down in casual shirt, shorts and sandals, looking very much at home in his native Cornwall. His office is spacious enough to house a Yamaha electric grand piano on which he treats me to a short burst of Gershwin's *Rhapsody in Blue*.

There's a blue sky outside and I've already clocked a beer mat on top of the piano inscribed with the words: 'I'd rather be sailing'. Richard keeps his boat in the enormous building next door that houses not only his heat-pump company but also the former showers used by the 250 underground workers here. 'This was the first building designed with metric measurements when the mine reopened in the mid-seventies,' he confides. 'It was considered state-of-the-art at the time and was described as the first "new" mine to open anywhere in the developed world in the latter part of the twentieth century.'

In fact, there had been a Mount Wellington mine on this site since the 1930s. Above Richard's desk is pinned a share certificate owned by the major shareholder, one Raymond Claude Neile Robinson, and dated 1935. 'The so-called "Robinson's Shaft" was just over there,' says Richard, pointing out of the window. Robinson died in August 1939, just before the outbreak of war, and work stopped a few months later due to lack of finance.

In its 1970s reincarnation, Mount Wellington was spectacularly unsuccessful. Largely because of water problems, the Canadian company that owned it managed to lose £10 million between 1975 and 1978, when it closed along with Wheal Jane. Temporarily, as it turned out. The two mines became one in the early 80s, soon after reopening, and stayed in business for nearly a decade.

It was rather different back in the 1930s when, as so often with near neighbours, the men of Mount Wellington and Wheal Jane chose to emphasise their differences on the sports field. 'There was an infamous rugby match between the two in 1937,' Richard confides. 'Thirty men walked on to the field but only five were able to walk off unassisted.'

When I tell this story to Alan Taylor at his house overlooking Truro Station, he doesn't seem particularly surprised, but prefers to emphasise the rather more cordial relations that had developed between the two mines by his day. 'We had a brilliant sports and social club,' he says. 'Our boast was that if three or more people wanted to do something, we'd organise it. We had an archery club, a ladies' netball team, a rugby club that toured Ireland and a tug-of-war team that were world champions at two weights,' he adds, wheeling himself across the room to look for a book with some photographs in.

Alan has no legs. But before you jump to any conclusions, dear reader, let me stress that his condition was the result of gangrene caused by diabetes. It's important for a former health and safety officer to point out that it had nothing whatsoever to do with mining.

Opposite, top: At one time the proportion of water being pumped to ore being brought up was 40-1.

Opposite, bottom: A forlon attempt to save Cornwall's tin mines.

GREAT ROCK

WE'RE GOING IN ANY MINUTE now. For the time being, however, I'm clinging to a branch while trying to maintain a foothold on a steep and very uneven hillside rutted with exposed and somewhat sinister-looking tree roots. In the trench a few feet below me, former mining geologist Bob le Marchant is applying WD-40 to the lock of a gate that was slammed shut in 1969 when Devon's last metal mine closed. At the time, Great Rock was the only source in the UK of micaceous haematite, a form of iron oxide used in rust-resistant paint. It helped to coat battleships in distant oceans and bridges across Sydney Harbour, Victoria Falls and the Great Western Railway.

Bob has a eureka moment when the lock finally gives way and the 4ft-high gate to one of the tunnels, or 'adits', creaks open. 'You're going to get wet feet. Is that all right?'

He's not kidding. I've watched the trickle of water issuing from the mine grow almost into a torrent. When I gingerly lower myself from my elevated perch, reddish water surges over the top of my totally inadequate hiking boots. It's soon up to knee level on my jeans. Ah, well. Miners all over the West Country were regularly wading to the rockface in conditions like this, and they had to do it every day of their working lives. So wade on, Macduff, or at least le Marchant. I'm right behind you.

We leave behind the warm sunlight filtering through the trees and duck into a world that would be pitch-dark were it not for the lamps attached to our helmets. Through the murky water we can just about make out the wooden sleepers of the extraordinary Heath-Robinson railway system that once conveyed blasted rock out of the mine. 'I wouldn't tread on any of that wood, if I were you,' says the echo-y voice in front. 'It's rotten, and there's a fifty-foot drop about there,' he adds, pointing a foot or so to our right.

Well, I'm glad you mentioned that, Bob. I make sure that I follow exactly where he leads as we edge our way around the hole and splash onward until something glints in the gloom. It's the ore that men, mostly from the nearby village of Hennock, used to go looking for every day. Bob inserts a finger into a lode, or vein, and out it comes, as soft as putty. But the lode is quite narrow and the miners had to chase it a long way back – up to 1,700 feet back, Bob reckons. They'd use explosives, creating adits off adits, climbing up ladders in places where the ore was plentiful and ultimately connecting one level of the mine with another. There were three or four levels, some 40 feet apart, from the bottom of the hill to somewhere near the top. Like the tin miners of Cornwall, the men here were burrowing into almost vertical granite. That's one of the major differences between metal and coal mining. Coal seams are predominantly horizontal.

Mining was once a thriving industry in Devon, a county more often associated with cream teas and dreamy lanes through lush countryside. The Great Consols Mine, on the Devon side of the River Tamar, unearthed copper and arsenic in the nineteenth

Inside the mill, 1945.

Washing plant and mine office, 1945.

and early twentieth centuries. At its peak it employed over 1,300 men. There were copper and tin outcrops, too, as well as lead and silver, around Tavistock on the west side of Dartmoor. Manganese was worked near the village of Doddiscombsleigh here on the east side of the moor. Some of the villages closer to Hennock also mined micaceous haematite during the first half of the twentieth century. One by one they closed down until Great Rock was the only one left. The nearby Kelly Mine went in 1951, but now has a preservation society dedicated to restoring it as a monument to Dartmoor's mining heritage.

It won't be reopening as a working mine any time soon, however. Nor will Great Rock for that matter. But why did it close in the first place?

'Simply because it became uneconomic,' says Bob. 'The lodes here are not much more than a couple of inches wide. In Austria they're more like a couple of metres in width, which obviously makes it far more accessible. At one time Austria supplied the German Navy with the mineral to paint its ships. Now it supplies the whole world.'

The frustrating aspect of this for a mining enthusiast such as himself is that there's so much ore still here. 'Look at it sparkling all around us,' he says. I do and it is. Every time I turn my head, the helmet light beams up another lode. 'I could fill buckets with the stuff,' Bob adds wistfully. 'I don't think they mined it particularly efficiently when it was open. These days you wouldn't need to keep blasting rock; you could use high-pressure sprayers to wash the stuff out. I'd love to start mining here again.'

He's one of those who believe that this country was built on mining minerals and making things, and he can't understand how we can survive by selling things made by people on the other side of the world and shuffling money about. So what's holding back his ambition to become a 21st-century mine owner?

For one thing, he knows that any proposal to restart mining would bring on an attack of the vapours among conservationists and those charged with maintaining one of Britain's national parks. 'Apart from that, I don't have the money and I'm too old.'

He's sixty-five, albeit as fit and sure-footed as a mountain goat, judging by the way he has led the way up and down this steep and wooded hill before we even ventured inside it. Earlier we've been round to the other side to look at the so-called Beadon workings, narrowly avoiding a head-on collision with a white-van man hurtling around twisting lanes narrow enough to accommodate nothing wider than a tractor. It was on this side of the hill, away from the main mine buildings, that the last five miners must have been working when Bob paid his first visit here as a young man in 1969, shortly before the closure. 'I was based at South Crofty [in Cornwall] at the time,' he recalls, 'and I came here on my bike. It was like the *Mary Celeste*. There was nobody around.'

And there had been nobody around today as we'd trekked through bracken and bramble looking for the ghosts of a mining past. 'They used to keep pigs at the mine,' Bob called back over his shoulder as I trailed in his wake. 'They were always escaping and I get the impression that some of the miners spent more time chasing pigs through the wood than they did looking for iron ore.'

We stopped for a moment and looked at the 'reservoir'. Not much more than a large pond, it used to power the water wheels before 1952 when that new-fangled electricity came to Great Rock. There were fish in the reservoir at one time and some of the miners apparently used the techniques perfected by Cretan fishermen – lobbing in the occasional stick of dynamite to blow them out of the water. Sticks of the stuff for blasting rock faces used to be delivered to the men as they took a break for a bite to eat in what was known as the 'grub hut' here on the Beadon Lane side of the hill. 'They had a little stove in there,' Bob recounted, 'and one day it caught fire shortly after the dynamite had been stored under the seats. The blokes were reluctant to go back in and try to put it out.'

Understandably so. They were miners and they knew what dynamite could do to a rock as hard as granite. As they looked on from a safe distance, the hut was blown to smithereens. The remains are still there – a rusted corrugated iron roof and some concrete slabs. Nearby, lurking in the underground, is a discarded Thermos flask with a distinctively mid-50s look about it.

By that time, the new mine manager Sydney Taylor had arrived and attempted to drag Great Rock into the twentieth century – not the mid-twentieth century, just the twentieth century. As we've learned, electricity had recently been installed and the make-do-and-mend philosophy of the Tuckers, foremen-cum-managers here for generations, was being challenged for the first time. 'Old Man' Charlie Tucker had been the first man in Hennock to own a car. Eventually he graduated from an Austin 7 to an Austin 10 in which, after a pint or three at the Palk Arms, he had a habit of driving through gates whether they were open or not. He also liked to stand on the seat, stick his head and his gun through the sunroof and take pot shots at passing rabbits.

These stories and many more are told in a book called *Great Rock, Devon's Last Metal Mine*, by Tony Brooks, a friend of Bob's and a fellow graduate of the Camborne School of Mines. I remember meeting Tony at the King Edward tin mining museum in Cornwall where he told me about the two weeks he spent working at Great Rock as a student in 1962. 'In fifty years of mining I've never come across anything like it,' he said. 'It was unbelievable how crude it was, like something out of the nineteenth century.' (And he had arrived, remember, long after Taylor had begun the modernisation process.)

In the book, Tony tells of his frustrating and humiliating encounter with that ingeniously improvised rock-shifting locomotive and his failed attempts to keep it on the rails. Having emerged from our close encounter with a Great Rock tunnel, emptied our boots and changed into dry socks and shoes, Bob and I are off to meet the man who built it.

Arthur Ball, now eighty-seven, lives in a village some five miles from Hennock. He has always lived there and he always cycled to work, for a 7 a.m. start, over the kind of hills that might draw sweat from the brow of Bradley Wiggins. When I ask him about the locomotive, he smiles ruefully. 'It was experimental at first,' he muses. Apparently he used a few 'bits and pieces' acquired from one Sammy Harris, the local scrap dealer. They included several submarine batteries, three or four starter motors from a lorry, an enormous chain drive, an Austin 7 gearbox and a tractor seat on a spring.

Not a great man for dates is Arthur, but his wife reckons he started work at Great Rock in 1950. 'There were no showers in those days,' he recalls. 'They didn't come in for another five years. You had to wash it off in the sink.' The 'it' in this case was the ore. The residue stayed on your skin and never quite came off completely, even in the showers. 'It glinted and sparkled on your arms so, when you walked into the pub, you'd get asked if it was raining,' Arthur smiles.

With his ability to make and mend just about anything, he became engineer and general factotum at the mine. His fondest memories include breakfast time, around nine-thirty, when the miners emerged after two and a half hours at the face. 'The office cleaner Sally Bradford – she was married to Sam Bradford, the blacksmith – used to put ham and eggs in the oven for them. Old Bill Wills, mind you, had a full dinner at that time: meat and two veg with a lot of gravy.'

The men took another brief break around one and finished their day at three. And, my goodness, they must have looked forward to knocking-off time. I was only inside Great Rock for twenty minutes, if that. But I shall always remember wading back, seeing the sun glinting through those rusted gates and thinking to myself: 'We'll be out any minute now.'

Iron oxide from Great Rock was used in rust-resistant paints coating bridges across the globe.

PENSFORD

CONSIDER THE CASE AGAINST the gus and crook, a device that was once commonplace in the Somerset coalfield. So-called 'carting boys' would have a rope harnessed to their waists with a long chain attached. The chain passed down between their legs and attached to it was a hook that was fastened on to a 'putt', the local name for a cart full of coal. Seams here in the southwest of England were particularly low, and these human pit ponies were used to drag what had been cut away from the face and into more accessible areas of the mine where it could be loaded into tubs.

Working conditions were among the most dangerous and unpleasant in the UK – difficult to equate with the county that also harbours the Georgian elegance of Bath, Taunton's picturesque cricket ground and an abundance of thatched cottages. Most people are surprised to learn that there was a mining industry at all in this neck of the woods. Ian McMillan, poet, radio presenter and a son of South Yorkshire, was so stunned to see a colliery spoil tip while being driven through the village of Paulton – 'It looked like a dormant volcano' – that he persuaded the BBC to allow him to make a programme about Somerset miners.

Sinking the shaft at Pensford Pit, 1910.

Now here's another surprise. You might imagine that the practice of tethering youngsters to heavy tubs of coal was something that died out around the time that it became illegal to send little boys up chimneys. You'd be wrong. It was still going on in 1949, two years after nationalisation, according to a display at the museum in Radstock, the town that had the biggest concentration of pits around it. By that time, admittedly, the 'boys' were more likely to be youths who had started working at the pit at fifteen rather than eight or twelve.

'It would still be better described as an instrument of torture,' insists Francis Hillier, chairman of the Somerset District Miners' Welfare Trust. 'Children were scarred for life around their waists. They used to try to harden their skin by rubbing in their own urine.'

A Royal Commission in 1928 failed to recommend calling a halt to this novel form of child labour, mainly because no miners came forward to speak out against it. 'They feared colliery closures and loss of jobs if it was outlawed,' according to Nick Turner, manager at the museum. Eventually it was Mavis Tate, MP for Frome, who succeeded where other well-meaning folk had failed. 'She was a Tory, which didn't go down too well with the miners,' says Francis. 'But she took a gus and crook to the House of Commons and evidently stirred things up. That would have been just after the war.'

Even then the practice didn't die out entirely. Rob Bailey joined Pensford, the most northerly of the Somerset underground collieries, in 1951 and recalls: 'It was still being used on the number-two seam to pull the rubbish [rocks, in other words] away from the airways.' But at least they weren't using children. 'The bloke who did it was a few years older than me,' he goes on. 'He would have been about nineteen.'

Pensford closed in 1958, by which time the workforce had fallen from over 400

to 250. 'It was too wet down there and there were too many faults,' says Rob, who went on to work at the Harry Stoke drift mine on the edge of nearby Bristol for a couple of years before moving to an animal feed transport company and working his way up to management. Now seventy-seven, he's a dapper chap with an immaculately pressed shirt and sunglasses protruding from the top pocket. But, like anyone who ever worked at a mine, he has never forgotten the experience or the men he worked with. 'Mining was a way of life, not just a job,' he says as we sit in the former Miners' Welfare in Pensford, at the far end of an enormous snooker table shrouded in a green cloth the size of a five-a-side football field.

'They used to hold dances in here on a Saturday night,' Rob tells me, 'and there'd usually be a punch-up at the end – two miners fighting over who was taking home the same girl. They'd be mates again on Monday morning. It was just that they'd had too many pints in the Rising Sun down the road.'

This being Somerset, there would have been draught cider as well as beer on offer in the pub. There was, by all accounts, a cider press in the village run by a local farmer. Miners would pick up a bottle on the way home from work to swill the dust from thirsty throats. 'You'd get it for free if you went to help with the hay-making when you came off shift,' Rob recalls.

Today we're drinking nothing stronger than tea or coffee, along with walnut cake supplied by the extremely hospitable lady from Thailand who runs the adjoining barber's shop. Francis has already availed himself of the opportunity to call in for a short back and sides before joining us. Also present is Bill Morris, secretary of the Miners'

Pensford Miners in the 1950s.

Trust, who started work at Pensford around the same time as Rob – except that he was on the weighbridge and later in the wages office while his pal was underground. 'When you left school in those days,' Bill confides, 'you either worked on a farm, at Fry's [chocolate factory in Bristol] or you went to the pit. We were told it was a job for life, but when I came back from National Service in 1955 they'd given my post to someone else.' So he moved on to the Coal Board's central pay office in Radstock and, eventually, to Kilmersdon, one of the last two pits in Somerset. It closed in 1973, by which time Portishead Power Station was switching from coal to oil. Forty years on and Bill can still recite the check numbers of almost every one of the 350 or so who worked there. 'I go through them if I can't get to sleep,' he confides.

This seems an opportune moment to explain that the check number was common to all collieries. Each miner was issued with a metal disc with his number on it. He would recite it when he went to the pay window to get his wages and he would hand over his disc in exchange for a lamp at the start of every shift. The disc would be given back when he handed in the lamp on his return to the surface. It was a way of checking that every man was accounted for. A missing lamp meant that someone was still down there, more than likely in need of a rescue party.

The chances of needing rescuing in Somerset were well above average, for reasons we've already touched upon. Imagine what a culture shock it was for Billy Grubb, who arrived in southwest England from Jamaica in 1953 and found himself working first at Old Mills, then at Norton Hill and Kilmersdon, sometimes up to his waist in water while breathing in clouds of dust. 'Conditions underground were terrible,' he told the

Somerset Guardian fifty years later. What's more, those low seams made the use of mechanised coal-cutters impossible in many parts. 'The roof would have shattered and come down on top of you,' says Rob. 'There was always a feeling of being squeezed. You felt you could be crushed at any time.'

It's hardly surprising that recruitment of local men became increasingly difficult at the dozen collieries that were still around at the time of nationalisation. Reinforcements came from mainly from Durham, Sicily and Poland. Well, to be strictly accurate, the Poles were already here. They'd fought alongside the British during the war and were unable to return to a homeland that was by then under a Russian rather than a German jackboot. 'They built three shanty towns of prefabs around Midsomer Norton to accommodate the Durham men,' Francis remembers.

And the Sicilians?

'They tended to live in Bristol and come here [to Pensford] on the bus,' Rob puts in. 'A lot of them went on to run restaurants there after the pit closed. They were the only blokes I ever saw wear plastic caps in the shower. They preferred to shampoo their hair at home. Took a lot of ribbing, they did.'

Now there's a surprise.

It's time for Francis to move on to another appointment. He may be in his late seventies but, as chairman of the Welfare Trust, he's still a busy man. Only the day before our meeting, the Somerset miners had held their 24th annual reunion at the Radstock Museum and some eighty men had turned up to enjoy a chinwag over 'a ploughman's lunch and liquid refreshment', as it said on the invitations. 'Michael Eavis was there as usual,' Francis reveals as he gathers his papers together. 'He's our president.' *The* Michael Eavis – the one who founded the Glastonbury Festival? 'That's the one. He's on record as saying there would have been no Glastonbury Festival but for New Rock Colliery.'

How come?

'Well, Michael was in the Merchant Navy when he got news that his father had cancer and the family farm was in danger of going under. So he came out of the navy and got a job on the face at New Rock [on the edge of the Mendips] where he was paid twenty-five quid a week. He used to get up at three in the morning to milk the cows, ride to the pit on a two-stroke motorbike, go home after his shift and milk the cows again.' The farm was duly saved for the family and, once Mr Eavis had discovered a slightly less strenuous way of generating income, for

generations of music-lovers.

It's soon time for the rest of us to follow Francis out of the Miners' Welfare. After profusely thanking the Thai hairdresser for her hospitality, Rob, Bill and I set off in my car for the site of their former place of work. Pensford Colliery was high on a hill, well beyond the borders of the village. It must have been quite a hike to work, I suggest.

'It was. And then you had to walk three miles to the face,' Rob points out.

The former winding house is now a private house – a very large and imposing one with a Mercedes convertible on the drive. The old canteen is now the site of a bungalow called The Bath House. At least the weighbridge where Bill started work is still there. So, too, is the former blacksmith's house, albeit totally derelict.

There's a fine view from here, right across the valley towards the Mendips on the far horizon. At the beginning of the last century there were nearly eighty collieries between

Left: Pensford Colliery from the air, 1950s.

Above right: The former Winding House, now a private home.

here and there. Beneath those idyllic-looking fields, men toiled in appalling conditions for coal owners such as the Beauchamp family, for whom Francis's grandfather was gamekeeper. Back in the nineteenth century, the Earl of Warwick owned land and mines in these parts, as did the Countess of Waldegrave. Managers sent regular payments to her London home at Strawberry Hill, Richmond-on-Thames – a long way from the filth and dust where young boys crawled around, chained to heavy tubs of coal.

What's harder to believe is that callow youths were doing the same thing for managers employed by a nationalised industry while the most radical Labour government that this country has ever seen was striving to build a New Jerusalem in England's green and pleasant land.

BIG PIT
(BLAENAVON)

FIRST I HAND OVER my mobile phone, then my watch. Car keys next. 'Anything else with a battery in it?' There is. I'd almost forgotten. Stuffed in another pocket is my voice recorder. No, we're not going through airport security en route to take-off. We're going in the other direction. Instead of soaring into the sky, we're soon crammed in a cage heading down into the Big Pit in Blaenavon. When I say 'we' I mean an excitable party of ten-year-olds from a Cardiff primary school, a couple of teachers and myself. Plus our guide for the morning, Russell Waite, one of several former miners employed here at what is now the National Coal Museum of Wales to give guided tours of their past.

Having briefly felt lighter in the pockets, I now feel considerably heavier round the waist, strapped as I am to a belt made weighty by the equipment necessary to power the light on my helmet. All miners went to work like this, for most of the twentieth century at least. They were also encumbered by the need to carry their own food and water. Not to mention lamps and the tools necessary to hack into rock faces and shovel away the sizeable lumps that came out of them.

Another big difference between our party and the working miners is that we're descending at a stately two metres per second. There would be more than a few screams today, I fancy, had we plunged down fifteen times faster. 'It used to be thirty metres per second when this was a working colliery,' Russell informs us in a matter-of-fact sort of way.

So our stomachs are still with us. But my scalp might have gone missing were it not for that helmet. I'm by far the tallest present and the one that has to bend forward most awkwardly when Russell shouts, 'Mind your heads,' before setting off down tunnels that are hardly 5 feet high in parts. At one point I raise my napper too quickly and take a fearful crack. Well, at least it gives the kids a giggle.

For them this is a school trip that they'll never forget into an alien, subterranean world that some of their grandfathers may have known all too well. After all, the South Wales coalfield was extensive and productive. And, as Russell has just reminded us, their home city was 'a tiny village' until the beginning of the nineteenth century. 'Cardiff was built up on the proceeds of the coal trade.'

Not half. By 1913 it had become the biggest coal-exporting port in the world. The First World War was imminent and the Royal Navy needed Welsh steam coal (maximum heat, minimum ash) in some quantities. Over 232,000 men were working in 629 mines turning out a combined total of 57 million tons of the black stuff.

Around the mountains of Blaenavon was a warren of drift mines with the wheel of the Big Pit towering above them. Although it was in old Monmouthshire, well to the east of what might be called the central coal belt of the Rhondda valleys, its steam coal was no less valued. Not long after the turn of the century, the local coal owners had

Previous page: Miners about to plunge down the Big Pit at 30 metres per second.

Getting changed for another shift at The Face.

sealed a deal worth well over a million pounds to supply French railways.

Until 1904 there had also been a voracious market much closer to home. Now part of the same World Heritage Site, the Blaenavon Iron Works had been sited just across the valley since the dawn of the Industrial Revolution and had been going full blast for much of the nineteenth century. From 1860 it had been fed by the Big Pit, which had six workable ironstone bands interspersed between the coal seams and mined separately. Inevitably there was some crossover and Russell has just handed the children a few lumps of coal embedded with iron 'pyrites' or sulphides. Not surprisingly, they're quite heavy. Given that I am the party's resident head-banger, the only surprise is that nobody has dropped one on my foot.

You could hear a pin drop when Russell reveals that children four years younger than these ten-year-olds were employed in mines across Wales, up to twelve hours a day, six days a week, until the Royal Commission report of 1842. They were known as 'trappers' and their job was to open and close the doors. For hour after hour they sat in pitch-darkness with a piece of rope tied to their wrists and tethered to the handles. At this point we're asked to turn off our lamps. All we can hear is the steady drip of water until Russell's sonorous voice chimes in through the blackness: 'These were the conditions that those children were employed in.'

It was necessary to open those doors at regular intervals to keep the downward flow of air from the shaft circulating through the mine in an attempt to prevent the build-up of methane gas. Unfortunately, it didn't always work, as Russell is about to demonstrate. While our helmet lights are still off, he sets off a small spark on a wire running along one of the tunnels. This was how the 'signaller' used to communicate with the 'engine man' from around 1910 onwards when electricity was being introduced to the bigger mines to replace horse-drawn haulage. 'It meant that two men could operate a system that had once required thirty pit ponies and hauliers,' he explains. 'Result: big increase in profits for the mine owners.'

It also resulted in a major loss of life at the Senghenydd Colliery, near Caerphilly, in October 1913. In this case the signaller's spark ignited a pocket of methane with appalling consequences. The final death count from the resulting explosion was 439, making this the biggest mining disaster in British history. It led to an underground ban on dry-cell batteries of the sort that power my temporarily confiscated mobile phone, voice

Top: Coal powered trains taking coal away.

Bottom: No longer any danger at the Big Pit.

recorder, car keys, etc. But even that didn't stop the disasters. Russell himself spent twenty-four years at the Six Bells pit near Abertillery where forty-five men were killed by yet another explosion in June 1960.

He doesn't mention this to the children, assuming perhaps that they've heard enough about the horrors of life underground. Nor does he go into great detail, when we finally arrive at what you might call the 'business end' of the mine, about what it was like to work at the coalface day in and day out. 'I could bang on about it for hours. Let's just say it was brutal, backbreaking work,' he confirms before going on to give us an informative insight into how the coal came to be there in the first place, fifty million years before the first dinosaurs.

There's pitch-darkness again in the cage taking us

back to the surface but, having been invited to give us a rendering of their school song, the children let rip with some gusto and no little harmony. Very Welsh. 'Did the miners sing on their way up at the end of the shift?' I ask Russell when we're alone.

He shakes his head before confiding, 'We were too bloody knackered.'

Operating the cage today is John Perrett, a Blaenavon man who still lives in Forge Side, the village on the edge of town built for the miners and iron workers. Now sixty-seven, he started work in 1963, first at one of many drift mines hereabouts and later at the Big Pit itself. 'I worked at the Garrow seam, which was between two-foot and two-foot-ten high,' he says. 'I was usually on my knees and sometimes on my shoulder. Very raw it was at the end of the shift,' he adds before giving a demonstration of how you swing a pick while lying down.

When he started, a shift was eight hours. It came down to seven and a quarter after the Wilberforce Inquiry of 1972. But that's still a hell of a long time to be working in such conditions. 'You knew when it was break time because the belt stopped,' he recalls. 'But you also had a good idea by the amount of coal you'd dug. Each man had ten yards of the face to work on and you were expected to put between ten and fifteen tons on the conveyor each day.'

John worked here until 1976 when he began training to be a deputy. The Big Pit itself lasted another four years, by which time the workforce was not much more than three hundred and fifty – almost a thousand fewer than it had been at its peak.

Men here also tended to be too tired to sing much by the end of a shift. John remembers: 'There was usually a bit of talk about rugby in the cage.' Especially, one imagines, when the Big Pit's own John Perkins was making his name as an intimidating second row with Pontypool. Voted one of the fifty hardest men in Welsh rugby, he didn't play for the national team until three years after his old workplace had closed.

There was a lengthy period when a veritable conveyor belt of men from the pits found their way into the Wales side. That's one of the big differences with the other side of Offa's Dyke where association football, rugby league or cricket were seen as the talented sportsman's way out of life underground. Cornish tin miners apart, rugby union in England was largely a game for former pupils of independent or grammar schools.

Ceri Thompson, who is now the curator here at the national mining museum, has a degree in Welsh history and literature from Cardiff University. But he spent the first sixteen years of his working life at Cwm Colliery. He was still working at the pit when he attended classes run by the Workers' Education Association in nearby Pontypridd. 'You weren't laughed at for doing that,' he assures me. 'After the pit shut [in 1986] I remember meeting an old miner on the bus. "What are you doing now, Ceri?" he asked me. When I told him I was going to university, his exact words were: "That's good. Show the fuckers we're not stupid."'

The 'fuckers', presumably, referred to anyone who wasn't a miner or, more likely, anyone who thought themselves above the miners. There has always been a long tradition of political radicalism among the colliers of South Wales. The Tonypandy Riots of 1910 and '11 forced them into wider UK consciousness when a young Home Secretary called Winston Churchill decided to send in troops to support the police. Long after the Second World War there were still Welsh miners around who, at the mention of Churchill's name, would deposit a black-flecked globule of spit on to the pavement.

One of Churchill's major political opponents, Aneurin Bevan, had worked briefly at Ty Trist Colliery, Tredegar, before moving on to become active in union and wider political circles. A brilliant orator, he will always be remembered as the chief architect of the National Health Service. 'He's supposed to have got his ideas for

Above: Children prepared
to enter the world of their
grandfathers.

Left: A 'cuppa' in the colliery
canteen.

the NHS from the miners' medical funds,' Ceri points out. 'They paid in a couple of pence a week to cover themselves for the cost of having to see the doctor.'

My visit to the Big Pit just happens to coincide with the day after the official report into the scandalous goings-on at the Mid Staffordshire NHS Trust and, after a bowl of soup in the former miners' canteen to the sound of Tom Jones's greatest hits, I climb into my car to find that Radio Four's *World at One* is giving the story almost as much coverage as the *Today* programme did at breakfast time and *The World Tonight* had the previous evening. As ever, there's no shortage of talking heads queuing up to give the impression that the NHS as a whole is irreparably broken.

I replace the radio with a CD (no, not Tom Jones) and head towards the Severn Bridge thinking about Bevan and the mining culture that forged his ideas at a time when politicians had some experience of real life before entering politics. God knows, the business of extracting coal from low and dusty seams was one that took its toll on limbs and lungs. But thanks to the vision and determination of a working-class man from Tredegar, the benefits of our generally still-impressive health service were not confined to the mining community or indeed to the South Wales coalfield.

HEOLGERRIG

Robert Haines' photography collection of Heolgerrig, *Once Upon a Time in Wales*.

TRUE TO HIS NAME, Christmas Evans would hand out pennies to the children of Heolgerrig every Christmas. Standing in the queue, hand outstretched, would be one Job Haines. As they used to say, look after the pennies and the pounds look after themselves. Many years later, that 'boy-o' had saved up enough to buy Evans's house. Mansion, more like. Heolgerrig House would have cost a pretty penny, even in the immediate post-war period, by which time Job was a mine-owner himself. Just for good measure, he also bought the Six Bells pub over the road and the small brewery next door. 'That's the site where my mother's bungalow is now,' says his grandson Robert Haines, gesturing out of the window of his four-by-four as we begin the ascent of the main road.

The old home town doesn't look anything like the same. Once it was a mining village, pure and simple. And the old miners' terraces are still there, lining this steep street with two chapels, the post office and the general store. But they're in danger of being vastly outnumbered by cul-de-sacs of three, four, even five-bedroom houses that are threaded around the hillsides and spreading across the grassed-over coal tips at the summit. 'Oh my God,' exclaims Robert. 'There was nothing like this last time I was here.'

Certainly the new houses were far less prolific five years ago when I was last here with him. Robert is a very talented photographer and documentary film-maker and I was here to write about the inspiration for his exhibition and book, *Once Upon a Time in Wales*, which was made into a film for French and German television.

The original black-and-white photographs had been taken, mainly in nearby Merthyr Tydfil, when he was twenty and home on vacation from his photographic arts studies at the University of Westminster. It was 1972, but these pictures could easily have been shot fifty or even a hundred years previously. Mufflered men with gaunt faces peered out from under flat caps. An old woman with a black shawl over her head was weeping into a grubby handkerchief as though waiting for news of a pit disaster. 'I could see that everything was changing . . . and I wanted to record some of the characters because we'd never see their like again,' Robert had told me at the launch of these retrospective portraits.

Pits had been closing all over South Wales since the First World War and his grandfather's drift mine, our ultimate destination today, had been put out of business in the mid-60s, seven years before the photography student embarked on shooting the past. Even in 1972 it would have been difficult to foresee what would come next: the widespread closure of the remaining shaft mines and the demise in 1987 of the last foundry in a town that had once boasted the biggest iron works in the world. Most of the factories have gone too.

These days the centre of Merthyr is dominated by a giant Tesco. Nearby is one of the few local institutions that haven't changed – not much anyway. The Station Café where I've met up with Robert again earlier this afternoon, still has pictures on the walls of local boxing heroes Howard Winstone and his trainer Eddie Thomas, a former miner who became British, Empire and European welterweight champion before guiding his protégé Winstone to the world featherweight title in 1968. Behind the counter is a coffee machine that looks as though it might have been cutting-edge in the late 1950s. (I once made the mistake of asking for an Americano, only to elicit the response: 'What's that when it's at home?')

Just round the corner on Merthyr's main street, the town hall is at last being handsomely restored. It was from the balcony here that Winstone waved to the crowds and Keir Hardie was proclaimed the first Independent Labour MP in Britain back in 1900.

Radical political thought was always stoking the smoky air in South Wales. Christmas Evans built Heolgerrig House in 1881 on the site of a timber-framed property where poets and radical thinkers used to gather. Chartist leader Morgan Williams was born there, and the red flag was raised there for the first time in this country.

So where did Christmas get his money from?

'From his father, Evan Evans, who started from nothing and opened a deep mine in the Rhondda,' says Robert. 'He was a man of humble origins, originally from Merthyr, who never spoke a word of English yet somehow acquired a substantial amount of land around Gilfach Goch.'

In 1868 he sank the Dinas Main Colliery, which was later connected to the Britannic. Dinas was renowned for the quality of its coke and coal. At one point, it seems,

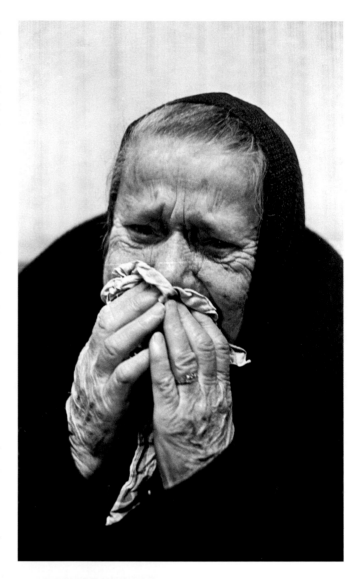

Evan Evans was employing so many men that he had to build a settlement to house them all. It became known as 'Evanstown'. Richard Llewellyn gathered much of the background material for his best-selling 1939 novel *How Green Was My Valley* from talking to mining families in this area. John Ford turned it into a film, starring Walter Pidgeon and Maureen O'Hara, in 1941.

The title, of course, was ironic. The valleys around here were anything but green. They were black. The same went for the hills above Heolgerrig in 1951 when Job Haines bought out Christmas Evans and moved his family into what inevitably became known as 'The Big House'.

As Robert recalls, 'There were gas-driven chandeliers, a servants' kitchen, marble fireplaces and a huge oak staircase with a stained-glass window at the top.' He ought to know, having spent the first eleven years of his life there. 'It was very draughty and quite scary for me in my early childhood. Mind you, there were tennis courts

and a beautiful rose garden outside, a pigsty round the back and a stable for Sally, the pit pony that hauled coal out of Granddad's drift mine.'

Gone, all gone. Not just the mine but the stable and the pigsty. They're now covered by portable cabins set up by Redrow Homes, the building company responsible for all these new houses. The tennis courts and the rose garden are under car-park tarmac and the Big House itself is now the Heolgerrig Club. It's closed this afternoon. We can just see the corner of a pool table through a contemporary glass-topped door at the side of the building.

At one time this would have been the miners' club and the concert room at the rear, now occupied by a community church, once hosted the young Tom Jones. 'The committee paid him off because they didn't rate him, apparently,' Robert confides. No knicker-throwing that night, one assumes.

Tower Colliery, which survived until 2008 because of the miners investing their redundancy money to keep it open.

We climb back in the four-by-four and head up the hill until the clouds look close enough to touch. A feeble wintry sun is going down behind the 'Aberdare Mountains' and failing to make any impression on the prevailing temperature. A vicious wind is whipping across the surrounding 'mountains', man-made from all the spoil to emerge from the many drift mines that riddled the hillside at one time.

The view from up here is spectacular. In the distance and to the left, there are more mountains – real ones capped with snow. Straight ahead the hills above Merthyr would appear to be alive with the sound of mechanical diggers (not that we can hear them from this distance). Coal was always close to the surface at the heads of these valleys and open-cast mining, using modern equipment and very few people, has resumed amid much controversy. Down in the valley itself, the show-jumper Sian Price (Robert's niece) is putting one of her horses through its paces. To the right of her, nestling in the hillside, is 'Crawshay's Castle', the substantial former home of the iron masters. Richard Crawshay (1739–1810) was a former London iron trader known to his workers in Merthyr as 'the Tyrant'.

Job Haines and his son Eurfil, it would seem, were far more highly regarded by the people of Heolgerrig. Certainly Robert was not bullied at school for living in

the Big House. 'They knew that my grandfather and my father had worked at deep mines in the Neath Valley before they came back here and started prospecting.' Invalided out of the RAF in 1947, Eurfil became a Bevin Boy who later went on to qualify as a mining surveyor.

The drift mine that the Haines family founded proved profitable for some years. They had contracts with several power stations, employing half a dozen men underground and another fourteen on haulage work. Robert remembers some talk about 'dodgy dealing' but, as a young teenager at the time, he's not sure exactly why they went bankrupt in the mid-60s.

He is sure, however, of the location of the mine that he used to visit as a child. 'It was just about here,' he says after we've eased our way through a gate threaded with barbed wire and plodded up a muddy track impregnated with tractor tyre marks. There are sheep around here somewhere, but they're probably sheltering from that wind. To be honest, I can't wait to get back in the four-by-four. But having established that there's nothing left of the family mine – 'that pile of rubble has probably been dumped here by a builder' – Robert is dreamily exploring his childhood haunts. Onwards and upwards we go until, at one point, I'm beginning to wonder if we'll soon be enveloped in cloud. For some of those miners who worked the many drifts around here it must have

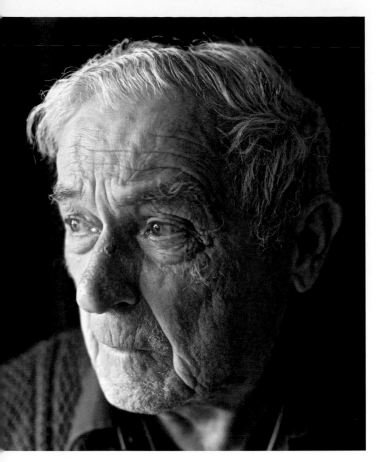

Left: Elwyn Jones, one of the few former miners still living in Heolgerrig today, caught on camera by Robert Haines in 2013.

been almost a relief to get underground on days like this.

'All the drifts here seemed to close round about the same time,' Robert recollects. 'Heolgerrig House had already been sold. We moved to the bungalow and my grandfather went to one of the miners' cottages.'

Mercifully, we're heading for one of those cottages any time now to meet one of the very few former miners still living in Heolgerrig. It's nice and cosy in Elwyn Marshall's living room. On the walls are framed photographs of sons wearing mortarboards at degree presentation ceremonies. In the other room is another photo of a granddaughter with a degree from Westminster College, Oxford.

Back in the front room we settle down in front of a very welcome gas fire. Elwyn gave up his right to concessionary coal in 1960 when he walked out of the Tower Colliery at Hirwaun in the Cynon Valley, just over the mountain from here, after an argument with a manager known to the men as 'Sackem Jack'. By that time he had done twenty years at the coalface, having started there a few days after leaving school at fourteen. This was wartime and men were in short supply. 'The Bevin Boys came in eventually, then the Irish and the Maltesers [men from Malta],' he says. 'We were working with picks for a long time, but eventually I was moved to a mechanised face.'

Was that easier?

'It was very hard work. There was only one yard of coal in a big face of rock.' So it must have been comparatively easy, you would have thought, when Elwyn moved to work on the production line at Hoover. But no. 'I couldn't settle at all. It was a different world. I remember asking a bloke next to me to hold a nut for me for a moment and he said, "It's not my job." You'd never have had that down the pit. I told him not to be so childish.'

Well, the Hoover factory closed in 2009 and Tower Colliery the year before – but only because nearly two hundred and forty miners had invested their redundancy money from the Coal Board and kept it going for thirteen years after the official closure.

Open-cast workings apart, the landscape round here is decidedly post-industrial now. On the way back to pick up my car from Tesco's car park, we pass another huge retail park near the A470 dual carriageway that almost certainly takes many of the new residents of Heolgerrig to work in Cardiff. Evan and Christmas Evans, Job and Eurfil Haines belonged to another world that existed once upon a time in Wales.

OAKELEY

YOU CAN'T GET AWAY from slate in Blaenau Ffestiniog. Blueish-grey slate (usually shiny with rain) on the roofs of mainly terraced houses; worn slate on the front steps; slabs of slate on mountains that look as though they've been turned inside out. The Oakeley Quarry here on the edge of town once housed the largest slate mine in the world, and it's difficult to tell where the natural mountains end and the spoil tips begin.

'A lot of muscle and tears produced that landscape,' former mine blacksmith Tom Roughead proclaims from our vantage point on the Crimea Pass, otherwise known as the A470. We can see wisps of cloud encircling the peaks. Here and there, sheep or goats can be spotted grazing high up on what look like perilously narrow ledges. The landscape, like the language the miners and rockmen spoke, is uncompromisingly Welsh. Everyone here in the northwest seems to be bilingual. Thankfully, Tom has effortlessly switched to English for my benefit.

'That part was known as the Quarry of Death,' he says, waving a finger towards yet another grey crag beneath which was an underground chamber. One of many. 'This one had clay between the veins and, when it dried out, things started moving. Any loud noise could bring a great slab of slate crashing down.'

As long ago as 1893 a government enquiry had found that the annual death rate for underground slate workers was 3.23 per thousand – higher than the rate for coal miners, and that was more than high enough. The so-called Quarry of Death, however, wasn't closed down until the 1940s.

By that time Welsh slate production was in sharp decline. Tiles were increasingly used for roofing. Between the outbreak of war in 1939 and the end of hostilities in 1945, the number of men employed in the industry in North Wales more than halved to just 3,520. (Fifty years previously there had been 17,000 workers.) And there was no immediate upturn when men came back from the forces. Although there was no shortage of bombed buildings needing repair, it takes time to work up production in an industry that had been largely abandoned. It seems that there was a brief revival in the early 1950s followed by a long decline. By then new factories were opening up in northwest Wales offering less hazardous and health-threatening ways of earning a living.

By that time, too, the famous narrow-gauge Blaenau Ffestiniog Railway had stopped transporting slate the thirteen miles to the coastal town of Porthmadog to be loaded on to ships. I ask Tom how high Blaenau is above sea level.

'Over eleven hundred feet.'

That was a hell of a gradient for train travel. Still is, of course, only these days the engine pulls passengers rather than slabs.

Not much more than 250 workers are employed in open-cast slate mining round here today, either in quarries or former mines that have had the roof removed like the top of a boiled egg. It's a far cry from the days when Oakeley was one of the so-

---

Miners dwarfed by the scale of their environment.

beyond doubt,' wrote Graham Isherwood in his 1988 book *Slate from Blaenau Ffestiniog*. 'The most experienced men had received the greatest exposure to the killing dust and so the dearth of experienced miners and rockmen increased.'

No wonder there are so few survivors around in the second decade of the twenty-first century. Of those few who are still with us, 'four have had strokes and two are not well', according to Tom. Despite suffering from Parkinson's disease and diabetes, he's fitter than most. Despite being one who mainly worked at a forge rather than the face, mind you, he was not immune to the hazards of slate mining during the nine years that he worked at Oakeley. Far from it, as we shall see.

The cosy home that he shares with his partner Ruth and an enormous dog is just across the road from the local X-ray department, and it was the wider availability of X-rays through the National Health Service that confirmed the scale of silicosis among slate miners in the first place. One wall of the living room is lined with books, Tom having been an Open University student later in life. He has a PhD in ancient technology.

Playing mutely on the television is an ancient

called 'big three' along with Votty, which was shut down in 1963, and Llechwedd, now a visitor attraction. Oakeley's underground workings ceased in 1970, although part of them were opened to the public two years later by Quarry Tours Ltd. Visitors continued to flock there until 1997 when the enterprise was sold to McAlpine's and the tourist side of the business was closed down. There is still some quarrying going on, I find as I pull off the Crimea Pass and we climb out of the car in the dying light of a November afternoon. 'See those gates,' says Tom. 'They're not the originals. The originals were hand-forged in 1914. Wrought iron they were. It took seven of us to lift them off when they needed repairing.'

A sign tells us that this site is now owned by Welsh Slate Minerals. But this is small-scale compared to what it was when it was a mine rather than a quarry and Tom started work here as an apprentice blacksmith just over fifty years ago. And it's nowhere near the size of the operation fifty years before that.

The writing had been chalked on the slate wall since the mid-1950s. 'All [the remaining mines] were but pale shadows of their former selves, their workforces ravaged by the effects of silicosis, a disease ignored for too long by many quarry owners until the evidence was

DVD of Ronnie Barker and David Jason in *Open All Hours*, which casts a somewhat surreal light on our subsequent discussions. On the hearth are a bronze 'rammer' and a brass horn. 'Someone blew that horn to warn everyone that they'd just rammed black powder into the places where they'd drilled,' Tom says, wielding both implements with some relish. 'Believe you me, it worked, and the men got out of the way at the end of the day. They'd come back in next morning to start clearing up, but only after the securers had been in to check each chamber of the mine and make sure there had been no misfiring.'

Needless to say, the black powder was an explosive, though somewhat less devastating than gelignite. Detaching slate in sizeable sections suitable for roofing was a rather more delicate process than digging out lumps of coal. Yes, there were slate miners whose job it was to drive through the headings or shafts to provide access. But there were also rockmen who worked in pairs. The one at the top could be suspended 120 feet in the air, abseiling across the roof of one of the many chambers. The one at the bottom had to ensure that the slab of slate that came hurtling down had a cushioned landing on soft clay before he set about chipping it into shape without

Opposite top: Welsh slate miners enjoying some fresh air in the distinctive landscape around Blaenau Ffestiniog.

Above: A welcome break to lay the dust.

Below: Slate wagon ready to roll.

Below: Is he a mountaineer or a miner?

chopping it into pieces.

As one of seven blacksmiths, it was Tom's job (once he was eighteen) to help maintain the chains on which the top rockmen were suspended and to keep the chisels up to scratch. 'There were eighty different veins in the mine,' he recalls, 'and the heads of the chisels had to be tempered differently for each of them.'

He was given an early taste of the hazards of mining when, aged sixteen, he was called upon to retrieve the missing arm of a man who had strayed too close to one of the belts in the mill. 'They had to get a helicopter to fly him to hospital in Liverpool,' he says, shaking his head as though trying to dislodge a particularly distressing memory.

Four years later he found himself peering into a tunnel where a man had been trapped by falling slate. His leg had been crushed. 'The old doctor who turned up was too fat. "You're the thinnest," he said to me. "You crawl in and give him this injection." I did and, thank God, he went out like a light.'

Tom himself was no stranger to the casualty ward. First he was involved in a cock-up with his boss in a scene worthy of Laurel and Hardy. 'We were welding a shaft over an open hearth when he spat on the anvil. Unfortunately, he missed, hit a piece of white hot metal, which promptly spat back and caught me just under the eye as I was in mid-swing. Instead of hitting the metal, I hit him – on the shoulder. Luckily it was the handle not the hammer head that caught him. But he still finished up in hospital in Llandudno, while I was sent to one in Bangor.'

Tom is able to smile about it now, but it can't have seemed too funny at the time. And worse was to come. Aged twenty-two, he was handed a rock drill and

assured that it was clean of any black powder. 'I started warming it up on the fire when there was an almighty bang,' he says. 'Only my leather apron saved me. My lung collapsed and I've still got the scars on my arm,' he adds, rolling up his sleeve to show me. 'Ended up in a chest hospital on the other side of Denbigh, I did. I remember the doctor saying, "The good news is that we've got your lung working again. The bad news is: you've got TB." Six months, I was off for.'

The wonder is that he ever wanted to go back.

'Well, in those days you just got on with it.'

For all the brutal realities of the work, there was a surprisingly civilised and cultural side to slate mining. Then again, perhaps it's not so surprising. This is Wales after all and this part of Wales in particular feels very different from the rest of the UK. The *caban* was the cabin where the men gathered for their lunch and the setting for wide-ranging discussions on issues such as religion, education and politics. Someone would be delegated to take formal minutes. A surviving set from 1908 to 1910 at Llechwedd records discussions on issues such as church disestablishment and tariff reform. But these semi-formal gatherings didn't die out in the early part of the twentieth century. They were still going on when Tom started work at the Oakeley in the early 1960s.

'We also used to have mini-Eisteddfods between the chambers at the mine – choirs, brass bands, even poetry,' he says. 'We blacksmiths had made a cup out of an old syrup tin and they competed for that.'

He's telling me this long after we've left Messrs Barker and Jason mouthing silently in his living room. We're driving down a main road at dusk to take a look at the sheer size of the estate once owned by Baron W.E. Oakeley, the man who consolidated various mines and quarries into a single operation in 1878. 'His granddaughter signed my papers to start work at the mine,' he confides. 'She was in her nineties by then and was still riding side-saddle on a black mare.'

Now there's a vision to conjure with. As we drive back, wisps of cloud are still circling around those grey peaks. It would be nice to report that I could hear the sound of ghostly choirs echoing through canyons of slate. But all I can catch on the drizzly breeze is the drone of cars passing by on the Crimea Pass.

GWYNFYNYDD

FORMER MINING PROSPECTOR George Hall will never forget the day that his team finally struck gold. 'I rang Sir Mark Weinberg to tell him and he said: "Take the boys down to the Golden Lion [in Dolgellau] and get them what they want."' Thirty years on and George can still remember having 'at least a dozen whiskies' and being conveyed home in a taxi. Heaven knows what the drinks bill was for him and the thirty 'boys' working for him. But Weinberg, the South African-born financier, evidently believed that they'd earned it.

Well, they had started drilling at Gwynfynydd early in 1981 and by the time they finally came across a vein thicker than a man's ring finger it was September 1983. 'In retrospect we were very close to finding it within the first three months,' George reflects. 'I remember us driving a tunnel into the quartz [the rock that sometimes harbours gold] and finding nothing. I was puzzled and disappointed because I'd done a lot of research and reckoned that was where it should have been. Still, we went off and searched elsewhere. As the months and then the years went on, I was becoming increasingly anxious thinking about all the money going down the drain. But Weinberg kept sending the cheques every month. Eventually we went back to where we'd started and I said to the contractor, "Try taking another three feet off this side."' Eureka! 'There was the vein.'

That's the way of it with gold, particularly here in the so-called Snowdonia Gold Belt. It's a very broad belt with well spaced out yet intensely glittery sprinklings of the sparkly stuff. As a former miner once said: 'Finding gold in most mines around the world is like finding cream in a sponge cake; finding Welsh gold on the other hand is like finding a sixpence in the biggest Christmas pudding you could imagine. There's no pattern, no logic and you never know when you're just inches away.' Or as George puts it, 'You either have a lot of gold or none at all.'

He's now eighty-eight and living in retirement on the edge of Ludlow in Shropshire. In his study-cum-library, shelf after shelf is lined with leather-bound books on mining. George has written extensively on the subject himself. The son of a cycle-shop owner from Gloucester, the extraction of minerals has been his abiding passion ever since he was conscripted to go down an iron ore mine in the Forest of Dean in 1943 (see New Dunn, page 69).

It was one of his own books written in 1974, a comprehensive history of Welsh gold, that attracted Weinberg's attention in the first place. 'He must have read the re-print because I was summoned to his office in Mayfair some years after the first edition and offered lunch,' George recalls. Over smoked salmon and white wine, Sir Mark popped the question: if George could reopen any mine in Wales, which one would it be?

There would have been quite a few options at one time. One might have been Dolaucothi in Carmarthenshire, opened by the Romans around AD 74 and closed in

Left: Dolgellau Mine 1880.

Below: A well earned break at Clogau.

1938. It's now owned by the National Trust. Another might have been Clogau St David's, near Barmouth, which had been Britain's richest in the early part of the twentieth century and had been closed and reopened many times since. It was finally abandoned in 1998.

George plumped for Gwynfynydd – 'partly because it had a lot of fractures that we could drill into and partly because it belonged to Frank Freeman, an old friend of mine, and I was fairly sure that he'd sell up for the right price.'

At this point, perhaps, a little history is required to put matters in perspective. The price of gold more than doubled during the 1930s to seven pounds per 'troy' ounce – a jeweller's term amounting to just over 31 grams in today's terms. 'That made mining more attractive and a man called Sale took over Clogau and Gwynfynydd,' says George. 'But he died in 1940 and with him the money dried up. Nobody had done too much mining in the post-war years. Frank [Freeman] put up some plant at both mines and things had just pottered on a small scale with one or two men getting a bit of gold out occasionally.'

The new riches emerging from Gwynfynydd in the 1980s enabled Weinberg to present the Queen with a kilogram of Welsh gold on her sixtieth birthday. 'That would have been worth between thirty and forty thousand pounds at the time,' George estimates. But didn't it belong to her anyway? Surely any gold and silver found in the rocks of 'this sceptred isle' is the property of the Crown. 'Yes, it is, except in the county of Sutherland where Charles II granted the rights to the Countess, one of his mistresses. But in this case the Queen's agents had let it to Weinberg as long as he paid . . . well, a royalty.'

He was getting plenty back once George and the boys had begun to repay

his initial investment. 'We were selling hundred-gram Nescafé jars to local jewellers for fifteen grand and sending him the cheques. There'd be other minerals in those jars as well, including calcite, lead and zinc. They weren't particularly clean. But I don't know another goldfield in the world with such high-grade ore.' Not even Tyndrum in Scotland, it would seem, where a company called Scotgold Resources recently started drilling again. 'It's much more evenly distributed up there,' he concedes. 'The frustrating thing about Welsh gold is that it's so intermittent.'

Ore or nothing, you might say. George parted company with Weinberg in the mid-80s and went off truffling for lead and zinc in the Lake District. But the Gwynfynydd gold rush, or at least the Gwynfynydd gold search, went on for some years after his departure.

It's now time for me to make my departure and head west. Eventually I find myself in the magical setting of the Coed y Brenin Forest Park. There's almost a fairy-tale quality about the idea that there was once a gold mine somewhere deep in the heart of the forest. These days it's just a big hole in the side of a heathery hillside. The lengthy, man-made track leading to it is bordered on one side by the River Mawddach, gushing and frothing over sizeable rocks, and on the other by the exposed mossy roots of trees in full autumnal splendour and hence bedecked in appropriate shades of gold.

This was John Humphreys' route to work, once he'd done a sharp left-hand turn off the A470 on the outskirts of the village of Ganllwyd. Not that he'd have had time to walk it. John was a fitter at the mine and, like the miners themselves, he travelled up the track by car – something you can't do these days. Mining stopped in 1999, partly because of the cost of meeting new health and safety controls and partly because of changes in pollution-control legislation affecting potential acidic discharges into the river. But it was kept going as a visitor attraction until 2007. These days the track is for walkers only beyond a certain point.

Sir Mark Weinberg arrived by helicopter when he paid a visit to his 'boys'. John remembers it well. 'He was a smart bloke in white overalls. Came into the mill and shook my hand, he did.'

The mill was hidden away underground to comply with the by-laws of the Snowdonia National Park. John worked there as a fitter, mending conveyor belts and crushers, and that suited him fine. 'It was warm in winter and cool in summer,' he recalls. 'Much better than being at the face.' His admiration for the miners is genuine. 'I can't remember seeing any broken legs or arms, but it's a wonder they didn't break their backs the things they were doing. Earned good money for it, mind. With bonuses they could earn between four and five hundred pounds towards the end of the eighties.'

Where did the workforce come from?

'There were Welsh, English and Cornish.'

Note the distinction. The Cornish saw themselves as a breed apart. Most had come from the tin mines, of course. Come to think of it, mining gold was a very similar process to mining tin – lots of drilling and blasting, followed by lots of crushing and sifting. 'You couldn't mine now with the machinery we used,' says John. 'Health and safety wouldn't allow it. Anyway, would you get the boys who'd want to do it these days?'

He thinks not, obviously. Apart from anything else, there were plenty of frustrations with gold mining in Wales, as we've already discussed – a lot of drilling and blasting for nothing. Then again, there could be surprises when you least expected them, as John remembers all too well. 'One day we decided to make the mill bigger to accommodate more tonnage. It meant taking a couple of feet off a rock pillar to get another conveyor in. One of the miners started shaving off the side of the pillar and there it was: four to five ounces of gold.'

He must have felt as though he'd just found the sixpence in the biggest Christmas pudding imaginable – valuable enough to buy a hell of a round at the Golden Lion.

Northern United Colliery deep in
the Forest of Dean.

NORTHERN UNITED

SOME FORESTS SOUND GRANDER THAN OTHERS. Deceptively so, perhaps. Most are straightforwardly named: Thetford Forest, Waltham Forest, Charnwood Forest, Sherwood Forest and the rest. Then there's the still magical-sounding Forest of Arden, immortalised by Shakespeare, and the *Royal* Forest of Dean. Plain old Dean Forest would sound more like a West Country folk singer or the blogging name of an eco-warrior with a vegan girlfriend and several nose studs.

Of course, the royal title was granted many centuries before bloggers or eco-warriors were heard of – for services rendered to more than one monarch. Indeed the so-called 'Free Miners' of this glorious Gloucestershire haven between the Severn and the Wye were first honoured by Edward I in the early fourteenth century, for playing a key role in recapturing Berwick-on-Tweed from the Scots, as it happens. Subsequent kings called upon them to fight in France during the Hundred Years' War. Henry V was particularly keen to have them as part of what Shakespeare had him call 'we few, we happy few' at the Battle of Agincourt in 1415.

Happy?

That's doubtful. But when the going gets tough, it must have helped to have tough men used to working in harsh conditions on your side. The miners from the Forest were known as powerful pullers of a long bow and fierce hand-to-hand fighters. They also knew a bit about digging trenches, installing stakes and undermining fortifications. Over a century later, in 1522, Henry VIII called on 300 men to travel from Dean to Dover for another fracas with the French.

By that time iron ore from the Forest had long been an important contributor to the national economy, having been mined here since long before Roman times. Under all these trees is a basin of limestone with substantial coal deposits overlaying the central part. Coal would be mined on a much bigger scale come the Industrial Revolution.

Today there are around 150 Free Miners left. Each was born within 'the Hundred of St Briavels (roughly equating to the Forest and surrounding parishes) over twenty-one years ago. Each will have worked a year and a day in a coal or iron mine 'within the said Hundred of Briavels'. And each has the right to open a 'gale', or mine-working, within the said boundaries. The Coal Nationalisation Act of 1946 gave specific exemption to allow this unique private privilege to continue and there are still around four gales being worked on a small scale today.

Somewhere in the Forest is the office of the Deputy Gaveller, charged with administering the scheme. National headlines were made in 2010 when John Harvey MBE, the incumbent at the time, allowed a woman to become a Free Miner (see next chapter). Cue disgruntlement among many former miners.

Not from Dave Harvey (no relation), however, the man who seconded her

Free Miners David Morgan (foreground) and father Robin, pushing the tram through the forest, 1994.

Forest, Northern United, which closed on Christmas Eve 1965. He has since become a poet, singer, all-round local personality and one of very few men to have not one but two statues modelled on his likeness while he's still very much alive and kicking. He's still a powerful-looking man, despite the wisps of white hair protruding from under a cap worn at a jaunty angle. There's a hale-fellow-well-met air about him and a readiness to engage in banter with passers-by, all of whom seem to know him and cheer up at the sight of him.

'How bist, old butty?' he greets me, and immediately I have the daft notion that I've wandered into a Dennis Potter play. It's a feeling that will recur at times during the rest of the morning as we judder through the Forest in Dave's battered old van on the way to the site of the pit where he earned his living and almost met his death. Sun is casting a dappled golden light on bracken browned by autumn, and the birdsong brings to mind the soundtrack to *The Singing Detective* – on those rare occasions when it wasn't overlaid by what Potter called the 'cheap' music of his childhood.

That most controversial of TV playwrights was a son of the Forest and indeed the son of a miner. Walter Potter worked at Cannop Colliery, among others, and Dennis was born in the village of Berry Hill in 1935. Dave was born there too, albeit three years later. 'I remember Dennis being the only boy in our school with a leather satchel,' he grins. 'My mate Terry got hold of it once, swung it round and let it go. It finished up high on the ledge of a building and we scarpered before old Walt came after us.'

Dave was evidently a bit of a lad in his day. He went to the same grammar

school as Potter but managed to get himself expelled in 1952. Later he became, by his own account, a 'drinker who got into scraps and sometimes went poaching'. These days he's a Baptist convert who lays off the booze. Public performances of his poems and songs, now available on at least two CDs, are popular events in the Forest.

In his anthology *Where We Belong* is a poem dedicated to Big Phil Bennett, the man who saved his life. The opening verse goes:

I remember down at Northern,
On a face called twenty-three,
How the roof of this long coal face,
Near squeezed the life from me.

And the eighth and final verse concludes:

Phil pulled me from this crashing roof,
The memory haunts me still,
I owe my life to this big man,
A giant called 'Big Phil'.

Left: Another load emerging from the forest.

Below: On the surface at Bixslade.

He was twenty-two stone, Dave reckons, and stronger than the average pit pony. Just as well that he was standing in the main roadway of the Northern United Colliery when the chain on the conveyor belt snapped and ripped out one of the roof supports. 'They were made of wood in those days [1963],' the pitman poet reminds me before going on to recount what happened next: 'I was two yards into the face when suddenly I was buried up to my chin with a piece of timber across my chest.' Dave pauses and smiles ruefully before adding, 'I thought I saw a bloke beckoning me through black gates with a fire behind them.'

But he was twenty-five at the time and Phil wasn't going to let him go to hell just yet. As verse six has it:

His arms under my armpits,
Hands clenched across my back,
This man he dug his heels in,
And I heard more timber crack.

Rather more prosaically, Dave goes on, 'I thought he was going to pull me in half. Since then I've had to have an operation on my spine. But the important thing was that he got me out and I was able to hobble to the pit bottom. Five minutes later the whole roof came down.'

Within two days he was back at the face. 'You'd lose your nerve otherwise,' he assures me. For some time afterwards, however, he suffered from nightmares. 'The doctor gave me sleeping tablets but all they did was to make the nightmares more intense.'

The statue that commemorates Big Phil's rescue was carved out of wood by Carlton Ryder, who works at the far end of the car park at the Dean Heritage Centre, near Cinderford. Phil himself is no longer with us. 'When I went to find him at his home in Mitcheldean to tell him about the poem and the carving, his wife told me he'd died six years ago.' Dave shakes his head sadly. 'Phil risked his life to save mine and I'll never forget him.'

Nor will he forget the other miners at Northern United. 'You weren't just mates underground,' he reflects. 'You drank together, played skittles, darts and crib together. The humour and the comradeship were like nowhere else.'

So it must have come as a considerable culture shock when he took a job as a lorry driver shortly before the colliery shut down. 'I could see the closure was coming,' he says. 'The other deep mines, Princess Royal, Waterloo and Eastern United, had already closed and

the water wasn't being pumped out. More and more was getting into our pit.'

So he swapped the cramped confines of those low, underground seams for life on the open road. A young man who had hardly ventured out of the Forest was travelling hundreds of miles every day. Alone. Instead of playing skittles with the lads, he might be stuck in a bed and breakfast just off the East Lancs Road.

It couldn't last and it didn't. 'My heart was still in mining,' he admits. As a Forester born and bred, it was time to exercise his rights. With his father supplying tea, sandwiches and a helping hand, he started drilling into the side of a hill at Bixslade some time in the 1970s. 'We used to be there till eleven o'clock some nights,' he recalls. 'It took a while, but eventually I saw the black stuff, and good stuff it was too. Eventually we had nine men working for us. Until 1980, that is, when the coal was getting awkward to bring up.'

The 1980s were a terrible time for miners everywhere, of course. That turbulent decade tolled the beginning of the end for the industry, and jobs paying anywhere near what miners earned were thin on the ground. Despite its 'royal' associations, Dean has been dubbed 'the working-class forest'. Today the beautiful surroundings can't quite disguise pockets of poverty. Some of the housing stock has seen better days. The 1960s *were* better days by far in terms of the availability of alternative jobs for people without much in the way of academic qualifications. 'After our pit closed, a lot of the blokes went to work for Rank Xerox in Mitcheldean or at the nylon spinners in Gloucester,' Dave remembers.

Opportunities for unemployed youngsters today are far fewer, as he's only too well aware. That's partly why he was a co-signatory with another former Northern United Miner, Les Ruck, to a letter to the *Forest of Dean and Wye Valley Review* in support of a controversial new road through their former place of employment. We're on our way to the site now – once we've visited Dave's other statue in the centre of Cinderford.

This one is the work of the distinguished sculptor Antony Dufort and is cast in bronze rather than carved in wood. Commissioned by the local council in 2000, it was dedicated to the miners of the Forest of Dean. Dave is depicted kneeling down with a pick over his shoulder, as though about to take a swipe at the window of the nearby Cheltenham and Gloucester Building Society. 'I was posing on my knees for about two hundred and fifty hours,' he reckons, 'and my knees aren't too good because I spent a lot of time on them at the coalface.'

So was all that posing worth it?

'Oh, yes. I'm proud to tell people that that's me.' Particularly on days like this, it would seem, when his likeness is unsullied by the misfortunes that can befall public monuments. 'I came here one morning and found a pair of ladies' pants on my head,' Dave says with a grin. Not for the first time today, an image of the young Alison Steadman revealing her soon-to-be-discarded French knickers in *The Singing Detective* comes to mind. Perhaps we should move on.

The site of the former Northern United Colliery is just up the road from the centre of Cinderford. A surprising number of mine buildings are still standing, considering. Considering that the shaft was sunk by the Crawshay family from South Wales back in 1932. And considering the pit has been closed for the best part of half a century. If some local campaigners have their way, the buildings will be standing for a while yet.

The proposed new spine road is part of a wider regeneration project and opposition to it falls mainly into two camps. One is concerned with conserving the site

as physical evidence of the Forest's mining heritage. The other is more concerned with preserving the wildlife. All kinds of species have made themselves at home here, including bats, newts and the small, pearl-bordered fritillary butterfly. 'Some of those environmentalists were in the paper the other day looking at some moth or other,' says Dave, shaking his head in disbelief before going on to point out the moss-covered roofs of the blacksmith's shop, the weighbridge office and, just visible through a clump of trees, the hut where they kept the explosives. 'A bloke used to come backwards and forwards with a hundredweight or so of gelignite on a trolley,' he adds. 'Not much thought about health and safety in those days.'

There is now, needless to say. Our visit has taken place under the close supervision of a security guard. I've since discovered that he's employed by the Home and Communities Agency to keep the public away from buildings riddled with asbestos. And there was me speculating that he and his colleagues were guarding the place round the clock to fend off a possible invasion by stop-the-road eco-warriors – Dean Forest to the fore.

Above, left: Another Free Miner emerging into the sylvan setting of the 'working-class forest'.

David Harvie looks at his spitting image in Cinderford.

Cannop Pit, the other side of Coleford. 'A world away from New Dunn'.

NEW DUNN

MEANWHILE, IN ANOTHER PART of the Forest, Dennis Gething is reminiscing about the days when 'it was all iron ore round here'. It was all fields too, with limestone beneath and trees above. Still is for the most part. The tiny village of Sling, a few miles to the west of Cinderford, doesn't occupy much in the way of acreage but, until the 1920s, it boasted two iron ore mines. The Old Sling Pit, as it was known locally, was closed soon after the First World War. It was connected underground to New Dunn, which somehow survived until the end of the next war. New Dunn was the last deep iron ore mine in the Forest of Dean.

An industry that had been around for thousands of years, covering an area from Lydney in the south to Symonds Yat, across the Herefordshire border in the far west of the Forest, had almost come to an end. Almost but not quite, as we shall see later. As in any form of mining, there had been peaks and troughs. Peaks included the Roman invasion, an improvement in charcoal-driven forges in the early 1600s and the coming of blast furnaces in the early 1800s. By the end of the nineteenth century, however, many mines had closed. The ore was thinning as the miners went chasing further into the depths of the earth. The deeper they went, the more problems there were with pumping out the acidic water that was responsible for iron deposits attaching themselves to limestone in the first place. There was also increasing competition from imports. Only the coming of what was to become known as 'the war to end all wars' provided a stimulus to home-grown demand.

Dennis is one of very few surviving iron miners round here. Certainly he can't think of many others. 'What about Harold Walker?' puts in his wife Bernice.

'He's died.'

'Oh, yes, I'd forgotten that.'

What she has never forgotten is a childhood memory of miners tramping to work through the Forest. 'The men in my family worked at Cannop Pit. I came from the other side of Coleford, see,' she adds, making it sound like the other side of the world instead of a mile or two up the road, 'and it was all coal in our part of the Forest. I wasn't even aware of iron ore until I married Dennis.'

That was sixty-one years ago. Dennis had started work at New Dunn nine years previously when the country was deeply embroiled in another global conflict. It was 1943, twenty-five years after the war to end all wars, and he was just sixteen. 'I remember it being very noisy, with all that drilling, and very dark,' he says. All he had to penetrate the gloom was a carbide bicycle lamp secured to his cap by a piece of wire. 'I had to supply that light myself,' he confides. It seems that the Watkins family, who owned the mine, wouldn't even run to a lamp, let alone a helmet. Perhaps they were already aware that the company was about to be taken over by the Ministry of Supply, iron ore being required as part of 'the war effort'. Soon after hostilities in Europe came to an end, the Ministry ceased paying the men's wages and the mine closed.

Before the war, the Watkins family had been supplying a foundry in South Wales. Iron from the Forest would eventually find its way into manhole covers and fire grates. Ochre was a by-product, and a comparatively profitable one. Known to the miners as 'colour', it was a powdery pigment found as a soft deposit intermingled with pockets of the harder, crystalline iron ore. It came in reds and browns, pinks and purples that were usually only available in synthetic forms, and it had to be scooped out. A railway branch line connected Sling to the so-called British Colour Works at nearby Milkwall where the ochre was processed for use in make-up or paint. The famous 'blood and custard' colours of the Midland Railway came from Forest of Dean ochre. 'There wasn't much of it left by my day,' Dennis recalls. 'At least I didn't see much of it.'

As a 'trammer', he would have been too busy pushing trucks along tracks to the pit bottom. 'It was hard going, but the blokes were good company and they looked after you. I was thin as a rake in those days, mind.'

Wartime rations must have been woefully inadequate for an adolescent doing a man's job, I suggest.

'Yeah, but it wasn't so bad in the country. My dad kept chickens, and some of the Free Miners in the Forest took up their right to keep sheep.'

He and Bernice still live in the former council house that he grew up in. But there was a period, from 1945 to 1948, when Dennis was slung out of Sling. Briefly he had become one of some 48,000 Bevin Boys, named after Ernest Bevin, Minister of Labour and National Service in the wartime coalition. They were mainly conscripted (some volunteered) to work in the mines rather than becoming soldiers. The 'boys' were really young men, aged from eighteen to twenty-five, though Dennis was still seventeen when he had the call from a man from the ministry – the Ministry of Labour, that is, rather than the Ministry of Supply.

'He wanted to send me to a silica mine in Scotland.' Silica? 'It was a kind of industrial sand used in firebricks. Anyway, I said to this bloke, "I don't think you can make me go." To which he replied, "Yes, we can, because you're eighteen on the day you travel." I spent my eighteenth birthday on the train to Bonnybridge and VE Night in Falkirk.'

By VJ Night he was in Perth. He was also in the army, en route to Palestine. Shortly after witnessing the turbulent birth of the state of Israel, he was back in Sling again. Rarely has W.H. Auden's phrase about the 'expansive moments of constricted lives' seemed so telling. He would go on to work in a variety of jobs,

including sand quarrying, dismantling boilers and 'making squash and Ribena just outside Coleford'.

The former New Dunn Mine used to be visible from the back of the Gethings' house. It now lies somewhere under an industrial estate on land still owned by the great-grandson of mine owner Fred Watkins. Among other companies, it harbours a steel and tubing stockist, a tyre fitter and the Taste Buds Diner.

This flat, edge-of-village site must have looked very different when George Hall knew it. He, too, was a conscript, though not a Bevin Boy. 'I was given a choice, he says. 'Join the army or go down the mines.' He chose mining and was 'lucky enough' to get a job at New Dunn in 1943, albeit on a different shift from Dennis Gething.

George cycled in every day from his parents' bicycle shop in far-flung Gloucester. Under his trousers was a pair of shorts, which he would wear for work along with plimsolls. Despite the recent installation of a powerful electric pumping plant, water still gushed around the third landing where he worked, and the shorts and plimsolls seemed to him a logical way of avoiding the discomfort of squelchy boots and sodden trouser legs. 'The more conventional Forest miners thought this was quite mad,' he told the NAMHO (National Association of Mining History Organisations) in 1999. 'And I found that my feet got so hot that I was under the necessity of standing in the running water when not otherwise engaged in keeping them cool.'

Like Dennis, he worked as a trammer at first and he makes it sound as though, at times, it was rather like trying to control a switch-back railway:

Aerial view of Cannop Pit.

A good stretch of track was very closely timbered, full of bends and on a steep gradient. In fact, the tram wouldn't quite clear the timber all the way and it required some trammers' arts to avoid knocking out a post or two on the journey. At the top of the hill we kept a few sprags [wooden pegs] to pop in at the back wheel as we went by, but I well remember shooting one straight through. This was towards the end of a shift and I had to descend brakeless and at alarmingly high speed, expecting at any second to demolish half a dozen pairs of timber and bring down the roof, or at least derail the thing and block the level with rock, which I would then have to reload pretty smartly. Actually I kept it on the line round a series of ultra-exciting corners, only to have it leap in the air on the flat, by the pit bottom and come to rest with one corner securely on the toe of my boot.

We must assume that by that time he had given up the plimsolls as a bad idea.

George is now eighty-eight and hale and hearty, judging by the strong voice booming down the line from his current home in Ludlow, Shropshire. Eventually he became a mining prospector. As recently as 1981, he helped to reopen a gold mine in Dolgellau (see page 56). But memories of life at New Dunn have stayed with him for over seven decades. After his tramming experiences, he eventually became a 'mucker', filling those trams with ore hacked from the limestone veins by the drillers – all hand-held machines in those days, apparently, with no 'airleg' support to rest it on.

His bonuses were usually measured in old pennies. 'But you were paid an extra five shillings [25p] a tram on those occasions when the drillers came across colour,' he tells me. 'You were part of a group and somebody senior decided who got what.' Like a 'butty' in a coal mine? 'That's right.' Unfortunately for George and everyone else who worked at New Dunn, the discovery of 'colour' was comparatively rare by 1943.

Ochre, however, is still being mined on a small scale at nearby Clearwell Caves – by a female miner, indeed. Elaine Mormon is the daughter of Ray Wright, a founder member of the Royal Forest of Dean Caving Club, who opened this 600-acre site of interconnected caverns and former mines back in 1968. She is also the only woman to become a Free Miner of the Forest (see previous chapter). 'I'm very proud of that,' she confirms, 'although it's caused a lot of animosity. Some of the other

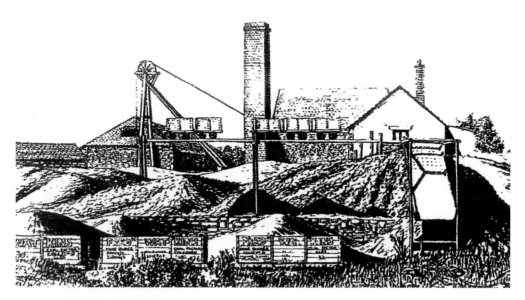

Right: Sketch of New Dunn just before it closed.

Below: Last miner out of Cannop Pit.

miners seem to think the rules have been changed to let me in. But I was born in the Forest.'

There's also a perception that she works at a tourist attraction rather than a proper mine, though she insists that she goes looking for those colourful pockets of pigment away from the underground paths that are open to the public. 'I enjoy it,' insists Elaine, a slim woman in her early fifties with a broad smile and a teenage daughter. 'It's hard, physical work and very good exercise. I use a small pick and sometimes a spoon to scoop it out. To be honest, there's not much ochre left now. Not compared to Canada, which has massive ochre mines. But there's enough for a mail-order business and some sales in our shop.'

Who buys it?

'Make-up companies, for the most part, and artists who want to mix their own paints. We also have orders from the army to buy the yellow stuff in raw form. They use it for painting tanks to blend in with the desert.'

Nearly 2,000 years on from the Romans first setting foot in the Forest, iron ore from 'round here' is still making a very small contribution to yet another war effort.

HIGHLEY AND ALVELEY

IT WAS ONE OF THOSE DAYS in England. One of those rare summer Sundays, to be more precise, when the sun shines and the English countryside dazzles. Few places look more ravishingly beautiful on days like this than the Severn Valley in Shropshire. Hikers, cyclists and fishermen are out in numbers. Some are gazing through binoculars to scan at close quarters the steep, green hills bisected by a broad, brown river. Can any of them tell that some of those hills have not been here for thousands of years? They're grassed-over spoil tips – legacies of the days when this valley was pockmarked by mines.

Coal being shipped over the River Severn by aerial ropeway.

Yes, there's coal in them there hills. Coal from Highley and Alveley Colliery, for the most part; coal that had been shipped over the river on an aerial ropeway and then rejected at the 'washeries' as not good enough to be sent up the railway line to the power station at Ironbridge.

That line is now part of the Severn Valley Railway, a magnet for steam train enthusiasts and visitors who simply want to enjoy a scenic journey via a quaint mode of transport. The view from the window would have been very different in the 1920s and 30s when there were quite a few pits in these parts – at Kinlet and Billingsley, Shatterford and even Arley, now an idyllic village that boasted a ferry across the Severn until 1964.

There was a ferry, too, linking nearby Alveley with Highley until the mid-1930s. Alveley miners had to pay six old pence (2½p) a week to be transported to the Highley side where the shaft had been sunk sixty years previously. Then the process was reversed. The coalface had shifted under the river. Highley was worked out and a new shaft had to be sunk on the Alveley side. It was the turn of the Highley miners to travel. A special footbridge was built in 1937 to enable them to walk to work on the other bank. Mining would continue there for another thirty-two years. It was finally abandoned because of geological problems, according to the National Coal Board, which abandoned exploratory plans to access the thick coal of neighbouring South Staffordshire before any underground connection could be made.

After that, men from both villages would have to travel considerably further to find employment. The days of walking over a footbridge would soon become a memory as distant as boarding a ferry had been for a previous generation. But at least there were still working carpet factories in Kidderminster and aluminium works in Bridgnorth back in 1969 when around a thousand miners were made redundant.

Having succumbed to what's known as 'concrete cancer', the footbridge was recently replaced by a new bridge close by. We're descending towards it now, Linda and Eddie Hirseman and me. Linda pauses and points across the river to a chimney just about visible above the treetops. 'That's where the pithead baths were,' she says. 'But for

some time after they were installed [with nationalisation in 1947] a lot of men would still walk home covered in coal dust. They reckoned it was bad luck to wash it off at the pit.'

Linda was born in a cottage on the Alveley side fifty-three years ago, and lived in another cottage close to the pit where her father was an electrician. Since leaving school she has done the accounts for the engineering firm based in what used to be the miners' lamp room. 'This is my world,' she beams, 'and I absolutely love it. As a kid, I remember the sound of pit boots clanking on the grating outside the lamp room where I now work. I remember the immaculate gardens that the Coal Board paid two men to maintain around the entrance to the colliery offices. And I remember the Christmas parties and pantos that they put on for us kids.'

She also recalls walking across the bridge to visit 'Granddad and Grandma' in Highley. Oh yes, and 'Uncle Gerald' coming back to visit her school in his MG sports car. He was better known to the wider world as Gerry Hitchens and he was my boyhood football hero. Scored forty-two goals for Aston Villa in 1960–61 when I was eleven going on twelve, looking on in awe from the Holte End with my mates or the Trinity Road Stand with my dad. No Villa player since has come close to scoring so many in a season. Hitchens should have played for England far more often than he did, but still managed five goals in seven international appearances. Then he broke the hearts of Villa fans by signing for Inter Milan for £85,000. Unlike Jimmy Greaves and Denis Law, he

Above: Gerry Hitchens a star in the making, front-row centre, on his way up.
Below: On his way back to see the lads at Alveley.

stuck it out in Italy for nine years, putting up with the food and the sun. Yes, he was kicked from pillar to post but, when you come to think about it, Italian defences must have seemed a doddle for a one-time Highley face-worker who cut his footballing teeth against former Clee Hill quarry men playing in pit boots.

'Uncle Gerald and Auntie Meriel were so beautiful that they could have been the Posh and Becks of their day,' sighs Linda. But their day was long before the dawn of celebrity culture and Gerry Hitchens was not a man to put on airs and graces. 'You don't know what hard work's like until you've been down the pit,' he was fond of telling interviewers, and he evidently never lost his respect for the men obliged to dig coal while he scored goals. He died after suffering a heart attack while

Child's eye view of Highley Colliery.

playing in a charity match in 1983. He was forty-eight.

Gerry's son Marcus is in Highley today for another charity football event. In weather more suited to cricket, he's among a sizeable crowd watching back-to-back games on the pitch where his father was first spotted by a scout from Kidderminster Harriers in 1953. Money raised will go to local cancer services. The occasion is the Stephen 'Paddy' Walford Memorial Cup to commemorate another local sportsman. Paddy also played for Highley and the Harriers as well as being a gifted cricketer with a batting average of 62.5. He was even younger than Gerry when he died, aged forty-four, in October 2011.

'It was lung cancer,' says his father, Graham Walford, 'though, unlike me, he never smoked. I used to wonder what it was like for Gerry's dad to lose a son while he was still alive. Well, now I know.'

Graham is seventy-one, a former coal merchant who used to deliver the fruits of the miners' labour. 'They used to say, "We're digging it and you're flogging it,"' he recalls, cheering up a bit at the memory of the banter that was part of life in the pubs and clubs of a pit village. And his broad, gap-toothed grin is a joy to behold when Marcus produces his father's England cap from a match against Brazil in the 1962 World Cup, plonks it on Graham's head and takes his photograph.

Dennis Bache, aged ninety, is sporting rather more run-of-the mill headgear in the form of a claret and blue Villa cap. Rather confusingly, he's wielding a wooden rattle in the old gold and black colours of Wolverhampton Wanderers. In his youth he apparently frequented Molineux as well as Villa Park. But it was a visit to the latter in 1950 that led to him being sacked from the colliery offices where he had worked for three years after being demobbed. 'The miners had booked a coach trip to watch a Monday afternoon FA Cup replay against Cardiff,' he recalls, reminding me that there were no floodlights in those days. 'Then they were going on to see Randolph Turpin fighting in Birmingham. Well, there was no way I was going to miss that. Trouble is, I was expendable and the miners weren't. They couldn't sack them because there'd be nobody to dig the coal.'

Undeterred, Dennis went on to become a coach driver for the local Whittle coach and bus company. These days he's known as 'Mr Highley' and there's even a pub called the Bache Arms in the village. When I ask him about Gerry Hitchens, he smiles with a mixture of affection and wistfulness. 'He used to come back to Highley regularly. He'd have a pint with the lads and we'd walk to Bridgnorth and back [eight miles each way] with the kids. He had a lovely personality. Nothing was too much trouble for him.'

Then Dennis points out Stan Jones, formerly of West Bromwich Albion and Walsall, one of several professional footballers brought up within a few hundred yards of each other on the same Coal Board estate. One of them, Ted Hemsley of Shrewsbury Town and Sheffield United, also played cricket for Worcestershire. I ask Stan what it was that made a Shropshire mining village such a sporting production line. 'The miners would come up from the pit, still black, play for half an hour on this pitch and let us kids join in,' he reflects. 'We learned more from them in five minutes than all the coaches in the world could tell you.'

The Miners' Welfare where they changed is now the Severn Centre, incorporating a gym, a swimming pool and a café serving full English breakfasts on an epic scale. Outside is a plaque commemorating the miners killed in the collieries of Shropshire between 1875 and 1969. Eight were from Alveley and nineteen from Highley.

Above right: The seams at Highley were only three feet high.

Right: Only the best coal was sent up the railway line to the power station at Ironbridge.

George Poyner, a carpenter and joiner who went down the pit every working day from 1942 until the close, points out the names of three men that he remembers falling down a bore hole in 1962. 'They were buried alive,' he adds ruefully. Others were badly injured in the cause of acquiring the fuel that kept the lights on in those days. Walter Smith, for instance, was pulled under an underground train when his 'snap' bag became entangled with it. He lost both legs. His brother Sam had his arm split open by a piece of falling rock. 'He was taken to Bridgnorth Infirmary where they used what looked like a scrubbing brush to clear away the coal dust,' says his grandson Ray Davis. 'Mind you, they were tough old buggers, those miners. Granddad would pull his own teeth out. Never went to the dentist. Eventually, he was left with what we called his "onion chaser". He used to follow a pickled onion around with his tongue and then pin it with the one tooth left at the bottom of his mouth.'

With George Poyner today is his son, David, now

Above: The Severn Valley Railway, no longer powered by coal from the Severn Valley.

fifty-one and a scientist at Aston University. He would have been eight when the pit shut and, as it happened, he went to Bridgnorth Grammar School. 'But had I been of my dad's generation, the pit is where I would have ended up; no question,' he confirms. 'You had to be entered for the eleven-plus and, if your parents couldn't afford the transport costs of sending you to Bridgnorth every day, that was the end of it.'

Bill Scriven is twenty years older than David and, when he was fifteen, he had two career choices. One was to work on a local farm, where he could have earned the princely sum of £1 17s 6d a week. The other was to become a miner on four quid a week. No contest for a teenager who knew he could triple his wages if he made it to the coalface by the time he was eighteen. 'Don't forget, though, that you had to give your mother half your wages. That was the norm,' he adds.

His mother and father kept pubs in Alveley: first the Royal Oak and then the ancient Three Horseshoes. In those days they were both obliged to close at three, just before the miners on the early shift emerged from the showers gasping for a pint. 'They made up for it after evening opening,' Bill recalls. His 'escape' from the pit came through a chance meeting with mining engineers who were staying for bed and breakfast at one or another of his parents' pubs. 'I got in with them and ended up going to Nottingham to train for their trade,' he says. 'I spent the next four years going round just about every coalfield in the United Kingdom, installing self-advancing roof supports. Miners were the same wherever you went. Different accents, that's all.'

Different coal seams as well. 'I've been down pits in Durham that went under

the sea and the seams were six-feet-six. They produced brown coal, though, that wasn't particularly good. At Highley the 'brooch' coal was much better quality, but the seams were only three feet high. The miners used to wear clogs and use them as their stool, like this,' he adds, kneeling on the carpet of his front room in Kidderminster and then sitting back on his heels.

We climb in his car and set off for Alveley. It's a wet Monday morning, six days before my visit to Highley, and the rain is relentless. On miserable and chilly days like this the chimneys of both villages would be issuing smoke from the concessionary coal that was a fringe benefit for miners. Bill remembers the laden lorries screeching up what was known as the 'pit bank' in first gear. 'They changed into second at the top of the hill just outside our pub and, because they didn't have much in the way of springs, the bags would tilt over, tipping coal all over the road. Old ladies would come out with shovels and scoop it all up. Better for it to be on the back of their fires than all over the road,' he adds.

As we drive past Alveley Village Hall and Alveley Cricket Club, he reminisces about the tensions between the two communities on either bank of the Severn at social and sporting occasions. 'We were the best of mates at work. Like all miners, we were dependent on each other. Whether you came from Alveley or Highley, it didn't matter. But we fought at our leisure. Some of those dances could be a bit tense, either at our hall or their miners' welfare.' When it came to football and cricket, it seems, local derbies here tended to be as competitive as anywhere else. 'There were some good fast bowlers around determined to knock a few heads off,' Bill grins. 'And football matches involved a lot of clogging.'

Back in the sunlit uplands of Highley the following Sunday lunchtime, the match between the Miners' Welfare FC and Alveley FC is played in a comparatively sporting spirit. It's difficult to tell whether that's because of the hot weather or out of respect to the Walford family or simply because 'kids today' are not as competitive as their granddads who worked down the pit.

There are handshakes all round, followed by a mass exodus to the working men's club, sited behind a row of Victorian red-brick terraces that might have come straight from the pages of D.H. Lawrence had they been on the other side of the Midlands. It feels good to be here, particularly after a hot pork and stuffing roll washed down by a pint of Hobson's Town Crier. Only one pint for me, alas. There's a long drive ahead and it's time, in the great traditions of British journalism, to make my excuses and leave.

Travelling back along those glorious summer lanes, I switch off *Test Match Special* for a while and think about the centre forward who set Villa Park and then the San Siro alight some fifty years ago. Gerry Hitchens could soar above many a craggy centre-half. But having met members of his family and so many people from the mining community that forged him, it's easier to understand why he always seemed able to keep his feet on the ground.

Above: The beautiful Severn Valley. Nobody would imagine that there was coal under some of those hills.

Far left: Alveley Colliery mines rescue team in 1938.

Left: A sculptor's tribute to Highley's mining past.

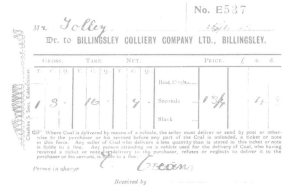

LITTLETON

I HAVEN'T BEEN in Chris Lilburn's front room more than a few minutes before I'm being called a 'bastard'. Not by Chris, I hasten to add. Nor by his wife Sheena who has just returned from the kitchen after making me a cup of tea. 'He's probably referring to me,' she sighs with a contemptuous glance at the African Grey parrot that has just uttered the insult with a cheerful chirrup. 'I hate him,' she adds by way of a weary explanation. 'He's always squawking when I'm trying to watch the telly and impersonating the phone when I'm in the other room.'

'He' turns out to be a she. A DNA test recently confirmed that, and a parrot once called Alfie is now known as Molly. But to Sheena she will always be a he. For all her choice language, Molly appears considerably less menacing than the Harris hawks that Chris kept until recently. Fed on dead chicks with a passing resemblance to gassed pit canaries, they looked as though they'd be more at home perched on a cactus on the Texas–Mexico border than in a small back garden in Staffordshire.

Last time I was here was five years ago. I was writing a piece for the *Guardian* about an exhibition by photographer Luke Unsworth, who had been brought up here in Cannock, and I wanted to find out what had happened to some of the miners that he had first photographed back in December 1993, when Littleton Colliery closed for the last time. Before we ask that question again, let's find out what happened to those hawks. 'The quarry where I used to exercise them was closed down and shut off, so I didn't think it was fair to keep them,' Chris explains.

Scanning the skies for birds was always a traditional weekend pastime for men whose working horizons were cramped and dark. Chris's dad was a pigeon fancier, like many a miner. 'He was part of the pigeon club at the White Lion down the road. I used to go there with him and put the rings on them before they were driven off to France or wherever. But once Dad retired from the pit, we never had pigeons again.' His son, meanwhile, developed a taste for rather more exotic bird life.

Lilburn senior eventually returned to Blyth, near Newcastle. Like a lot of Geordie and Scottish miners, he had migrated south in search of work when local coal seams had been worked out. The Geordies brought with them not only a passion for pigeons but also the technique for growing corpulent leeks that had to be zealously guarded against sabotage on the night before a competition.

'My dad was a great leek grower,' Chris confirms. 'I was about six months old when he moved down here,' he adds in flat West Midland tones. He's fifty-two now and has been in and out of work since having to leave Littleton Colliery with a persistent spinal condition. Ironically, he had to call it a day in 1989, just a few years after joining the national fight to win miners the right to work. At Littleton he was one of around 200 strikers out of a workforce of over 2,000 who stuck it out for a year. What kept him going? 'The spirit of the other lads and the thought of my dad. He'd have gone mad if I'd gone back.' (His father, then in his eighties, made it on to regional television in the

Northeast after being arrested soon after joining a picket line.)

In many ways Chris is the antithesis of the archetypal militant miner that those in the pro-Government media at the time liked to portray as Arthur Scargill's storm troopers. This morning he's wearing an England away shirt under his zip-up jacket and sporting a couple of chunky earrings in each lobe. Former workmates toot horns or wave to him from front gardens. A popular bloke, then, and it's easy to see why. He's easy-going with a good sense of humour and, when I ask him what he misses about the pit, he replies initially with a two-word Irish expression: 'The craic.' Then he expands a bit: 'Since

beyond a patch of muddy waste ground, is the main A34 flanked by modern housing and a few shops. Gone is the pay office, the lamp room and the pithead baths. 'They were supposed to put one of the old pit wheels outside that new school, but it hasn't happened yet,' says Chris, pointing to a building that looks more like a stadium than a place of education.

Unlike nearby Lea Hall, which closed even earlier, Littleton was never dubbed a 'super pit'. It was, however, deemed to be a 'core' pit by the then Conservative Government in 1992. A year later it was closed down and nearly 600 people lost their livelihoods. Scant thanks, you might think, for breaking the million tons of coal mark for

Previous page: Returning to work after the strikes.

Right: Increased output by Littleton miners made no difference to the ultimate fate of the colliery.

Far right: Chris Lilburn in the days when he kept his hawks.

leaving I've worked in factories and on building sites, but you never get the same humour, the feeling of being together. It was a dirty and dangerous job and your life depended on the man next to you.'

Before going back to the house for my encounter with foul-mouthed Molly, we've been up to have a look at the site of his former workplace. Chris's Vauxhall Zafira comes to rest on the edge of the car park of a doctor's surgery called the Colliery Practice. The name is just about the only recognition that there was a thriving coal mine here just twenty years ago. All we can see,

two years running and having a tonnage per man-shift way above the national average. By that time, it should be remembered, the Central Electricity Generating Board had long been following a government-driven policy of looking for sources of power other than British coal.

Here in South Staffordshire the seams were around 6 feet high. 'But in places they went right down to not much more than the height of that fence,' says Chris, gesturing to the exterior of the car park where a wooden rail stands well under 3 feet. 'You had to crawl on your belly for maybe two hundred feet through mud and everything.' Everything? 'Water that had been there for millions of years – dinosaur piss or whatever. If it got on your skin, you felt it burn. It stung until you had a shower and, when you got home, it was still blotchy. The nurse at the pit would put cream on, but it did no good. The blotches stayed for about six months. Eventually they gave us oilskins like the fishermen have. But you didn't really want to put them on. It was so hot down there.'

Dangerous, too.

'I remember seeing a big piece of sharp rock come down and go through the shoulder of the bloke in front of me like a bacon slicer. I just reached forward and pushed his skin back on. At the time we were working

within'. The one that ended with humiliating defeat for the National Union of Mineworkers.

'We got our arses kicked,' admits Chris Stewart, another of the Littleton miners who stayed out for the full year. He was in his mid-twenties at the time and paying his mother £20 a week for board and lodging. 'She was a Tory,' he says. 'She was always telling me how wrong we were to be on strike.' That must have led to some lively arguments, I suggest. 'You didn't really argue with my mother. Let's just say we had ongoing discussions. Truth is, I was brought up a Tory, but the pit changed me. It showed me how things really are. I miss the blokes I worked with. The humour was merciless. You have to be

under fields halfway to Stafford. It took us about forty minutes to get him back to the pit bottom and into the lift. And to do that we had to ride on the conveyor belt for a while. The nurse took him to hospital where they stitched him up. After a few weeks he was back at work.'

Such a working environment forged close bonds that were severed in some parts of the country, including Cannock, by the divisive nature of the miners' strike. *The strike* – the one that lasted a year, pitted neighbour against neighbour, police against pickets, national government against what Margaret Thatcher chose to label 'the enemy

careful what you say at the places I've worked since.'

There have been plenty of them. After being refused a job at Daw Mill Colliery in Warwickshire – 'We don't want you lot with your funny ideas,' the personnel manager informed him – he has worked at Birmingham Airport (twice), a drop-forging works in the Black Country (since closed), a chocolate factory in Telford, the Peugeot plant in Coventry (closed) and an incinerator in Wolverhampton. He is now employed at a nearby power station largely fired by coal imported from Russia and Indonesia.

Chris is fifty-two with a wife and three children. 'I didn't get married until I was thirty-eight, so I had it easy compared to some of those I was out on strike with,' he reflects. 'They lost marriages and houses and, in some cases, their lives through the pressure of it all.'

When I ask him about his politics now, he replies: 'Left-wing, but not part of any grouping. Let's say I'm very similar to Fazzer.'

Fazzer is Sean Farrell, the former NUM official also known locally as 'Young Scargill'. Well, he was only twenty-one when, as he put it, he 'led from the front' on the picket line at Littleton. He's forty-nine now, so has he mellowed a bit?

Yes and no. There are times when he comes out with statements that might arouse a round of applause at a Conservative Party conference. 'Work is a moral obligation,' he proclaims. 'At the pits we had a community with a purpose. The vast majority wanted to work. Now we don't have a working class much any more. We have an underclass quite prepared to stay at home and stick their hand out for benefits.'

At the same time, there's no disguising his

Above: Littleton Colliery alive and kicking.

Below: After its demolition, just the outline remains.

bitterness about what was done to his industry and his comrades back in the mid-80s. And his ability to analyse and argue is as formidable as it was when he first confronted eminent Conservative Sir Norman Fowler when the MP was still a member of the Thatcher cabinet. It was not long after the strike and Young Scargill had briefly become a football hooligan. 'The police had already criminalised thousands of us as an instrument of the political decision to get rid of the NUM,' he told me when we first met five years ago. He had been an unusual member of Wolverhampton Wanderers' Yam-Yam Army insofar as he carried a copy of the *Guardian* to away matches and travelled first class on the train if he could get away with it.

Plain Mr Fowler, as he was then, must have been a little apprehensive when the former NUM official sat down opposite and suggested they have a little chat. By the time they were coming into Euston and the cabinet minister had managed to escape, three onlooking businessmen had given Sean a points decision, he maintains. 'They didn't know that the union had given me a good political and economic education on day release at Keele University.'

Five years on and he's taken time off from his ice-cream van – yes, the former union hard man now trades under the name Mr Softee – to meet me at one of those 'family friendly' pubs that offer, among other things, a 'Kids' Carvery' for the under-tens. At least it's handy for the station, which, come to think of it, is probably why he chose it as a venue.

Sean surprises me again by calling for a pot of tea instead of a pint, startling the barmaid by speculating out loud on the size of the file that he is convinced that MI5 built up on himself and other activists. Then he sits down to expound views that seem bracingly at odds with the bland background music. Whether you agree with him or not, he has thought long and hard about the events that transformed his working life and those of many more former members of what used to be known as the working class.

'Our communities were devastated purely on political grounds,' he maintains. 'To me it's no coincidence that the Big Bang [the deregulation of financial markets] occurred just after the NUM was defeated. The enemy we faced was organised and ready for the fight and they had a long-term vision. Their strategy was well thought out. It was to take out the elite troops first in the expectation that the rest would crumble.'

When I ask him how he feels about those who felt

obliged to go back to work before the strike was over, he is surprisingly sympathetic. 'No workers in this country have ever been exposed to the kind of pressure the state put on the NUM. The banks squeezed mortgages, the government's friends in the media turned people against us and the police were used as a force against us. Those who went back are human beings and they just cracked. It was in September and October 1984 that real financial hardship started to bite. They'd been out all summer. And I know they went back to work with a heavy heart. We saw blokes cross the picket line in tears. I don't hold a grudge against any of those lads. In fact, I went into business with one of them two weeks before the pit closed. Fair play to all of them. At least they didn't lie down on the floor of coaches like the three hundred here who "scabbed" all the way through.'

Patrick McLoughlin was one of the Littleton NUM members who chose to work from the start of the strike. He's now MP for Derbyshire Dales and, after a spell as Chief Whip for the Conservative Party, David Cameron appointed him Secretary of State for Transport – one with an intimate knowledge of coach travel in turbulent circumstances. Back in the mid-80s, he was a 'darling of the right' at the Tory conference as one who stood out against what he would see as intimidation from militant pickets in his own union. Messrs Farrell, Stewart and Lilburn have all mentioned him to me at different times. Were they gathered together around a table in anything other than a 'family pub', it's possible that mention of Mr McLoughlin's name might just add a few more expletives to the vocabulary of any African Grey parrot with its ear cocked to the wind.

The Queen's donation to the Hamstead Colliery disaster in 1908.

HAMSTEAD

ON A SCORCHING AUGUST DAY in 1963, Frank Forster left his native Northeast with his wife and three daughters and moved south to work at Hamstead Colliery. That's Hampstead without a 'p'. As far as I know, there were never any pits on Hampstead Heath in northwest London. This Hamstead lies on the northwest frontier of Birmingham where it blends into the Black Country. The local paper is the *Express and Star* rather than the 'Ham and High'; you're unlikely to bump into Melvyn Bragg or Glenda Jackson in the newsagent's, and the most exotic eating place is a curry house in a row of shops on the Old Walsall Road.

All the same, this is no run-down former mining town. For the most part it's semi-detached suburbia, almost rubbing shoulders with Handsworth Wood, one of north Birmingham's more affluent districts. 'It's difficult to believe now but there used to be an overhead wire carrying a succession of buckets from the colliery to the Hamstead Brick Works,' Frank assures me. 'They were full of stone that had been separated from the coal. Chipping off the stone was my first job on the surface when I started work at Monkwearmouth. I was fifteen.'

He was eighteen when he moved to the coalface and twenty-four when he upped sticks and moved to the Midlands. Fifty years on and he still sounds more Sunderland than West Bromwich. And, yes, he still supports the team whose current Stadium of Light looms over his previous place of work.

'The football banter used to be a bit lively when anything up to twenty men climbed into the cage at Hamstead on a Monday morning,' he recalls. 'There'd be Albion and Wolves fans, Villa and Birmingham, Sunderland and Newcastle, Rangers and Celtic all wedged in together.' Cardiff and Swansea as well, I shouldn't wonder. 'Oh, yes, there were loads of Welshmen at the pit. But it didn't matter where you came from when somebody farted. That always changed the conversation. Nobody would ever admit to it, but there was usually more than one culprit. Most of them had had a weekend on the beer and the atmosphere could be pretty stinky in that cage.'

Not that they were in there for too long. Astonishingly, this had been the deepest coal mine in Europe soon after it opened in 1876. The coal was nearly 2,000 feet below the surface. But that cage plunged to the pit bottom at 60 feet per second. Frank was used to it by the time he'd moved south. 'The first time I went down Monkwearmouth I had to go back again to collect my stomach,' he grins.

Migration from Scotland, Wales and the northeast of England towards the centre or the extreme southeast had been going on for decades. The irony in Frank's case is that Monkwearmouth stayed open for another thirty years after he left, while Hamstead closed down two years after he arrived. 'They'd promised us forty years of work,' he shrugs.

There was no shortage of coal under Hamstead. Even today there's reckoned to be millions of tons of the stuff down there. The problem was getting at it. 'Too many

Above: Waiting for news, 1908.

Far right: More memories of the disaster that took twenty-five lives.

faults,' says Frank. Displaced seams, in other words. The pit's geology had engaged some of the finest engineering brains at the National Coal Board's disposal. Back in the 1950s, indeed, a deputation of mining engineers from Philadelphia had visited Hamstead to inspect the colliery's new-fangled hydraulic roof supports.

The NCB did its best to find work for as many as possible of the 800 or so miners made redundant by the closure. Frank went first to the Baggeridge Colliery in nearby Sedgley and then to Hilton Main on Cannock Chase. One closed in 1968, the other the following year. 'That's enough,' he said to himself. He spent the last twenty-three years of his working life first making and then analysing brass castings at a factory in inner-city Birmingham. Was the work easier? Silly question.

'Oh, God, yes.'

At least there were plenty of manufacturing jobs in the West Midlands in the 1960s. 'I'd grown up on the banks of the Wear,' he muses, 'and there were two choices: mining or shipbuilding. Through my bedroom window I could hear all that banging and bashing in the shipyards and I thought to myself, that's not for me.' So he finished up at a coalface a mile under the sea. Did that bother him? 'Never thought much about it. My dad worked three miles away and once we met up underground and had a brief stint working together. But the seams were low, no more than three feet, and there was always a feeling that the coal was going to run out. I wanted a more secure future for my young family.'

Arriving at New Street Station half a century ago was something of a culture shock. 'We'd never seen such tall buildings,' he confides. Nor had they ever clapped eyes on people from the Caribbean or the Indian subcontinent. The Forsters caught another train to Hamstead Station, a few stops from New Street on the Walsall line, wondering what to expect next.

Just around the corner from the station and close to the No. 16 bus terminus is a comparatively recent and distinctive addition to the otherwise featureless surroundings. It's a memorial to the twenty-five miners and one rescue worker who perished in a terrible fire at Hamstead Colliery in 1908. This sizeable and appropriate tribute was unveiled a century later by Professor Carl Chinn, local historian, radio presenter and columnist whose undiluted Brummie tones have been a feature of the airwaves in these parts for some time. But the man who began the fund to raise the money was Reg Hackett, former chairman of the Hamstead Tenants and Residents Association. 'I married into a mining family,' he told me over the phone from somewhere near where we're standing now, 'and my brother-in-law Bill Bowen was crushed between two tubs underground in 1958. Before she died, I promised his wife that I'd organise some kind of memorial to the miners of Hamstead.'

Looking down the list of names of those who perished in 1908 is rather like looking at a First World War monument in a French village. Members of the same families are listed. Here, for instance, are three Summerfields. 'All brothers,' Frank confirms. One mother lost three sons because someone left a candle burning in the wrong place.

As the twentieth century wore on there were further reminders here, as elsewhere, of the risks that miners took to unearth the source of power to keep the electric lights burning above ground. Leslie Brownhill's brother Eli and his workmate were gassed underground, having been cut off by one of those many faults on 28 May 1937. 'Eli was the family breadwinner,' Leslie, now eighty-six, recalled from his home in Cradley Heath. 'My dad had retired from the pit and I was only eleven.'

There are reminders, too, of other deaths in a room dedicated to the former miners at the Tanhouse Community Centre halfway up Hamstead Road. It's while

we're looking at the displays in there that Frank casually drops out that he knows what it's like to be buried alive. 'They always used to say "keep your timber in" – your roof supports in other words. Stupidly I didn't do it one day. It took three men twenty minutes to dig me out. I was unconscious for two or three minutes and, when I came round, I thought I was a goner. Luckily there were no breakages, but they wanted me to go to the surface to get treatment for the cuts and bruises. I knew that if I went off the face at that point, I'd never feel able to go back again. So half an hour later I was back at work.'

Those old miners were tough as teak. Frank is now well into his seventies but has a vigour and energy that you so often sense with men who once pitted themselves against the elemental forces of nature underground. He leads the way to the key sites of the former mine with a jaunty stride.

As Max Boyce never quite sang, the pithead baths are a petrol station now. There's a car wash, too, which means that motorists are swilling the grit from their Ford Sierras or Peugeot 207s on the spot where miners once scrubbed the dust from each other's backs. 'The baths is also where they paid us our wages,' says Frank. 'The pithead itself was across the road,' he adds, pointing through the passing traffic to the sides of some 1970s semis. 'We used to get there across a bridge like one of those walkways over the motorway. Then we'd be into the lamp room where you picked up not only your lamp but two check numbers. You handed one in and you took the other with you. That one you handed in at the end of the shift so they would know if anyone was missing. Before we went down, everyone was frisked for cigarettes and, more importantly, matches. Smokers had to chew tobacco or snort snuff while they were underground.'

As for food or 'snap', that was wrapped in a piece of paper and hung from one of the girders by wire or string. 'Trouble is, it was sometimes full of holes by the time you got a break.' Mice? Frank nods before adding: 'You were so hungry by that time that you ripped out the holey bits and ate the rest anyway.' He's telling me this having just made me a ham sandwich and a cup of tea at the spick-and-span council house where he and his wife Sheila have lived for fifty years on what used to be a colliery estate. The local authority apparently paid the princely sum of £1 to buy each house from the Coal Board not long after the closure. 'Today, me and Bobby Walker are the only two former miners still living here,' Frank reflects, pointing out the Walker household as we set off back to Hamstead Station.

Above: Rescue workers waiting to go in.

Opposite top: The last miner to be rescued.

Opposite bottom: The memorial unveiled by Professor Carl Chinn, about a century after the 1908 disaster.

How different it would have seemed half a century ago. Every one of these houses would have been occupied by mining families from all over the UK. The main breadwinners would have argued passionately about football over beer that many of them were still getting used to. And, yes, they would have complained bitterly when one or the other broke wind in the pit cage. But beneath the ground they were a band of brothers, united by the difficulties and dangers they faced in a fault-ridden mine that was once the deepest in Europe.

Traditional panning for salt was hot and thirsty work.

ADELAIDE

Think of salt mining and what comes to mind? Siberia, perhaps – generations of Russian dissidents shivering, shovelling and suffering alongside common criminals in conditions that those of us from more temperate climes can only struggle to imagine.

Now think about the salt mines of Cheshire and Worcestershire. Yes, Cheshire, with its rolling farmland, its prosperous towns and villages housing Manchester United and City players, *Coronation Street* stars and descendants of Mancunian cotton magnates. And Worcestershire, with its gently undulating countryside, its atmospheric county cricket ground, its abundance of handsome half-timbered buildings and its setting as the home of that yeoman family keeping most of us in touch with the goings-on of rural England: the Archers.

Salt-mining has gone on in other parts of the UK, and still does at Carrickfergus in Northern Ireland and on Teeside as a by-product of potash extraction. But the main centres of salt production in this country have always been around the 'wich' towns of mid-Cheshire – Northwich, Nantwich and Middlewich – and, to a lesser extent, around Droitwich in Worcestershire. Although 'wich' is a derivative of the medieval word for salt, the search for the stuff was going on a long time before the Middle Ages. Salt is, after all, a product fundamental to human existence. We may consume too much of it these days, but we'd be unable to function without it.

Over the centuries, salt has been the cause of wars and has served as money; hence the term 'earning your salt' and the very word 'salary'. What's more, there are over thirty references to salt in the Bible. The Book of Genesis assures us that Lot's wife was transformed into a pillar of salt. It was divine retribution, apparently, for looking back longingly instead of dutifully fleeing with her husband from the doomed depravities of Sodom and Gomorrah.

Droitwich and Middlewich, comparative pillars of probity both, were known to the Romans as Salinae because of the brine springs they harboured. And the road from Droitwich to Hanbury (one of three villages thought to be the inspiration for Ambridge in *The Archers*) has always been known as the Salt Way, according to my local informant and self-confessed mining 'enthusiast' Kelvin Green.

We'll catch up with Kelvin later, but first we're off to Northwich. More specifically we're going to Marston, on the edge of town, to the site of what appear to be two large lakes divided by the old road to Warrington. They're not natural lakes at all; they're 'flashes' – the flooded remains of former rock-salt mines that are part of the landscape round here. This one was known as the Adelaide and was Northwich's last salt mine. It closed in 1928. 'There would have been between forty and fifty men working here at the time and, when it started to flood, they obviously felt it wasn't worth maintaining,' says Tom Hughes, education officer at the Weaver Hall Museum, formerly known as the Salt Museum.

The watery grave of the former mine would be almost idyllic, as dusk draws on,

Above: The redder 'beef salt' looked like something that could be carved up as the Sunday joint.

Right: Sunset at the flash, where the Adelaide salt mine once stood.

Below right: Salt mining still in operation at Winsford Rock Salt Mine.

were it not for the traffic thundering through. On one side a cormorant is swooping low over a clump of reeds. Through a brief lull in the lorries and cars we can hear filtering through the slightly misty, fading light the sound of cows lowing from flat and distant fields. Beyond the flash on the other side of the road, the physical remains of Northwich's salty heritage are more in evidence. The far shore is dominated by the rusting corrugated-iron exterior of the New Cheshire Salt Works. It was taken over in 2005 by British Salt, which trades under the rather more familiar name of Saxa. Production is now centred on Middlewich, six miles down the road. There they evaporate and process the raw material pumped from the Holford brine fields on the other side of Northwich.

We've passed the pipes on our way out of town. 'They go the other way as well, twelve miles to Runcorn to be processed for the export market,' says Tom. 'The salt goes to Germany and other places and a lot's used in the chemical industry.'

We've also passed the former Lion Salt Works by the side of the Trent and Mersey Canal. Plans are afoot to turn it into another museum. The business closed in 1986, by which time the traditional method of open-pan salt making had long been modified to cause far less damage to the environment. A hundred years previously the centre of Northwich had come close to sinking as a rising tide of brine began to undermine the very foundations of its buildings. Only the formation of the Salt Union (of employers rather than employees) in 1888 brought some

order to the chaos being caused by the frantic search for salt by small-scale operators. And only the importation of so-called 'balloon-frame' building methods from Chicago – essentially a comparatively modern form of timber-framing – brought some order to Northwich's increasingly higgledy-piggledy High Street.

The new wooden buildings could be 'jacked up' again, unlike the old brick ones that were leaning and lurching at alarming deviations from the vertical. An American visitor in 1902 wrote about 'quaint little Angel Inn' as having 'not a straight line in it, vertically or horizontally. The floors are wave-like and no windows are plumb.'

Not surprisingly, the Angel is no longer with us. Like many another part of the Bull Ring and High Street, it didn't survive the so-called 'Big Lift' initiative of 1920 to 1924 when the buildings had to be raised back to street level. One consequence is that the Weaver Hall Museum, sited slightly away from the town's central core and built as a workhouse in 1839, is the second oldest building in a town that can trace its history back some two thousand years.

Panning for salt began with the Romans and continued on a very small scale until the 1960s. By that time the pan houses had been largely replaced by the much more efficient vacuum evaporators as a way of converting brine into salt. Panning had peaked a century earlier, just before the 'Great Subsidence' of Northwich. Having been pumped to the surface, brine had to be heated in pans that could be anything up to 20 feet by 8 feet. The key figures here were the 'lumpmen', who worked extremely long hours. They were responsible for keeping the furnace going to dry up the water and leave fine salt crystals to be raked to the side of the pans by the 'wallers'. Quite often the wallers wielding those heavy iron rakes were women – the lumpmen's wives for the most part, as a factory inspector revealed to a horrified commission of enquiry in 1876. What horrified them was that the women sometimes stripped down to their petticoats because of the fierce heat they had to work in.

By the standards of Victorian England, conditions in the deep-shaft rock-salt mines were comfortable compared to the pan houses and indeed to other types of mining. They were 'dry with good head room and a pleasant, even temperature all the year round', according to a pamphlet written for the museum by one Mary Rochester. 'The ventilation was adequate, although in the hot weather stale [gun] powder smoke could linger in the mines. There was no gas or sudden roof falls as in the coalmines. However, the presence of large quantities of explosives for blasting, and the use of naked candle flames to ignite the straw fuses, meant that danger was never far away. Candles were used for general lighting in the mines and the introduction of electric light was strongly resisted by the miners who preferred the traditional tallow candles which they stuck in the rock face when they were working and firmly believed gave them a better light.'

Compared to brine pumping, rock-salt mining has a short history on these shores. It started as recently as the 1670s when employees of the Smith-Barry family were looking for coal. Instead they discovered salty rocks under the grounds of Marbury Hall, the family pile near Northwich. It seems likely that there would have been some of the reddish mineral known as marl in whatever they unearthed. Certainly the clear, icelike appearance of pure salt is a rarity in Cheshire. Most of what emerged from the mines, after blasting and pick-axing, had a distinctly pink tinge. There was also the redder 'beef salt'. As its name suggests, it looked like something that could be carved up as the Sunday joint.

Perhaps it's time to move from the past tense into the present. Rock-salt mining still continues on a large scale at Winsford, five miles down the road from here. What used to be known as the Meadowbank dates back to 1844 and claims to be the oldest working mine in the UK. Not that it has been working continuously since those first shafts were sunk. Having been closed since 1892, it only reopened again after the brine flooding into the Adelaide began eating away at the salt pillars holding the roof up. That, remember, was in 1928, when the last of Northwich's nigh-on forty rock-salt mines disappeared in a flash.

The salt coming out of Winsford would have been exported to Australia, New Zealand and other overseas markets for cattle licks. After the Second World War, however, a new market developed closer to home. As our road system has expanded, so has the demand for salt to keep the traffic flowing on icy days, and Winsford is the main source of supply. Five hundred feet under the fertile fields of the Cheshire Plain are some 138 miles of tunnels. The salt face is ten minutes from the bottom of the shaft – travelling by van, that is. These are huge tunnels, supported by pillars of salt far thicker than Lot's wife, and the face itself goes back 80 feet. No blasting and shovelling is required. Since 2002 the process has been completely mechanised. A huge gauging machine scoops salt out of that face at a rate of a million tons a year. As a result, the people who work here are not miners but electricians, engineers and geologists. Oh, yes, and the three men required to keep that fearsome gouger working round the clock.

Working life would have been very different at Worcestershire's one and only rock-salt mine. But then it had a comparatively short life in the early 1800s. We're looking for its remains now, Kelvin and me. Remember Kelvin Green? He's the mining enthusiast who I mentioned briefly before embarking on the tale of brine-pumping and salt-mining in Cheshire. We meet up the day after my trip back from Northwich, a journey involving no fewer than five trains. This time I travel by car, parking up behind a fine-looking pub called the Bowling Green to which I somehow think we'll return after our brief sojourn around Stoke Works, not far from Droitwich.

The village was built by one John Corbett to house workers in the thriving salt works that he built up here after someone known as a 'brine diviner' was imported from Cheshire in the 1820s to verify likely sources. There were brine springs and wells all over this area and it was Corbett who also turned Droitwich Brine Baths into one of the most popular spas in the country. My late father-in-law used to travel down there from north Birmingham on occasional Sunday mornings and float around like a

tourist in the Dead Sea. Reckoned it was good for his rheumatism. He'd have been sad to hear that the baths closed in 2009.

I ask Kelvin where he thinks this rock-salt mine was?

'Something tells me it was around there,' he says, pointing to the gateway of a private home called Great Western House, lying between two elevated loops of the main Birmingham to Bristol railway line. He's come to this conclusion after studying articles by local historian A.F. Nicklin and the eminent geologist Charles Hastings. Nicklin maintains that the shaft was 50 yards due east of the derelict brine well in the southeast corner of the railway bridge. 'Well, we've just walked under the bridge,' Kelvin reminds me as the 12.42 from New Street to Temple Meads thunders overhead. 'And I reckon that's the capped brine well,' he adds, pointing to an ancient slab protruding from the brambles at the bottom of a wooden fence that has seen better days.

Above: Salty subsidence takes its toll on Northwich.

This is not idle speculation. Kelvin has, by his own admission, been obsessed with mines since his first and best-loved job, working for a Worcester-based company of mining engineers that became another casualty of the miners' strike of 1984–5. Researching and visiting old mine workings is his hobby – along with playing rhythm guitar and singing in a folk band called Celtic Connection. (Today he's sporting a Fairport Convention T-shirt under his jacket.)

He has already sent me a copy of Hastings' article 'On the Salt Springs of Worcestershire', which suggests that the rock-salt mine was sunk around 1828 and survived for not much more than ten years, almost certainly done for by the close proximity of the brine well. So what became of the salt works?

'It became an ICI chemical plant for a while,' Kelvin tells me, 'but that's gone now.'

What's known as the Corbett Business Park stands on the site, I notice, as we pass by on our way back to the Bowling Green. All this talk of salt is making me thirsty. A pint and a cheese cob are called for.

'Any chips with that?' asks the landlady.

'No, thanks.' I'd be tempted to shake salt all over them. Not good for the blood pressure. That's the thing about salt: we can't live without it and we won't live very long with too much of it.

BRYN HALL AND BICKERSHAW

John Dawber died in 1945, the same year that saw the closure of Bryn Hall, the colliery where he worked. He was in his mid-forties, the mine much older. The cause of death was put as bronchitis. Premature bereavements were not uncommon in the Wigan coalfield before nationalisation. It had one of the highest mortality rates in the country. Mr Dawber's daughter Jacqueline was obviously very young at the time she lost her father, but she still has his death certificate as well as the 'coal-cutting papers' that qualified him to handle one of those new-fangled electrically driven machines. They're dated 28 April 1936.

In the second chapter of *The Road to Wigan Pier*, George Orwell describes the coal-cutter as being like 'an immensely tough and powerful hand-saw, running horizontally instead of vertically, with teeth a couple of inches long and half an inch or an inch thick. It can move backwards and forwards on its own power, and the men operating it can rotate it this way or that. Incidentally it makes one of the most awful noises I have ever heard, and sends forth clouds of coal dust which make it impossible to see more than two or three feet and almost impossible to breathe.'

Mmmm. Could all that dust have been the cause of John Dawber's 'bronchitis' by any chance? More than likely. It also seems likely that he would have been working at Bryn Hall (or Crippin's Mine, as it was known locally) before qualifying to operate a coal-cutter. So he could well have been one of the miners whose physique, resilience and astonishing work rate the writer so admired. There's no doubt that this was the pit that he describes so graphically in chapter two. His diary entry from 24 February 1936, now lodged at his archive in University College, London, confirms it.

In the book, published just over a year later, Orwell makes the underground workings at Bryn Hall sound like the seventh circle of hell. He marvels at the ability of the 'fillers' – kneeling down in not much more than kneepads and clogs – to break up the huge lumps deposited by the electric cutter and shovel them on to the conveyor belt ('a glittering river of coal') at a rate of two tons an hour in stifling heat and dust overlaid by ear-bruising levels of noise.

Just getting from the cage to the face, over a mile away, was enough to leave the writer exhausted, with aching limbs and a sore back. Now Orwell was a tall man, exceptionally so among the industrial working class of pre-war Lancashire. But, as he points out, the tunnels were lower than 4 feet in parts, making it 'a tough job for anybody except a dwarf or a child' to get through without banging their heads or their backs. Or both. 'This is the reason why in very hot mines, where it is necessary to go about half naked,' he writes, 'most of the miners have what they call "buttons down the back" – that is a permanent scab on each vertebra.'

Fishing near Bickershaw Colliery in the 1930s.

Mining once dominated the landscape around Wigan. Bryn Hall Colliery, c.1945.

The Road to Wigan Pier was written ten years before nationalisation brought significant improvements in safety standards and working conditions, including higher roadways. But the fundamentals of coal mining remained the same and it makes you wonder why anyone who had read Orwell's first-hand report would want to go down the pit.

Well, Alan Davies had read it and he, too, is well over 6 feet. He's also an educated man, a former grammar school boy with eight GCE O levels and six A levels. 'Not very good grades, mind you,' he says, almost apologetically. Good enough, along with his interest in art and design, to get him into art college in Bristol. He stayed for a year. 'It sounds corny but I became a bit homesick,' he reflects. 'I didn't realise how much a rough industrial area such as this one meant to me.'

So he came back and worked first at Parkside Colliery in Newton-le-Willows, then Bickershaw in Leigh, both part of the Metropolitan Borough of Wigan.

'Parkside was a massive, fairly modern pit, only sunk around 1959,' he says. 'There were thousands of men there, many of them brought in from different coalfields where the pits had shut down. They tended to keep together with their former mates underground. There wasn't the camaraderie that I found elsewhere. Like Coventry, for instance.'

Coventry? What sent him to Coventry?

'My partner, Helen, was studying art there and, in those days [the early 1980s], you could go to any coal mine and say "there are my qualifications" and they'd find you a job. Eventually I got one on the face. The blokes there were from every part of Britain [see page 179] and at snap time we were constantly laughing at each other's accents. There was a great atmosphere.'

Anyway, perhaps we should get back on the road to Wigan Pier – or at least the road past Wigan Pier on the way out of town. The pier itself has always been a bit of a music-hall joke and even the museum named after it

big adventure.' He's fifty-seven and has a licence to fly a Piper Cherokee light aircraft, making him one of the few people who seem to be as happy 3,000 feet or so above ground as 3,000 feet below it.

At one time he would have had to fly over the 'Wigan Alps', as the range of sizeable slagheaps were known. Those man-made mountains once defined the landscape round here, as Orwell recounted with lurid fascination. There were six enormous heaps on the outskirts of Ashton-in-Makerfield, near Bryn Hall. 'The three left have been rounded off, reduced in height and re-christened The Three Sisters,' Alan points out.

Bryn Hall is our ultimate destination today. On the way we're following a Ford Fiesta with a back-window sticker assuring any potential miscreants: 'No pies are left overnight in this car.' Savoury pies were always a local delicacy in Wigan itself, home of the World Pie-Eating Championships.

We pass through town after town in what we might call Greater Wigan, each with its own mining legacy. The street names are flat-vowelled and monosyllabic – Plank Lane, Platt Bridge, Slag Lane, the latter lined by some of the posher houses in the locality. A fair percentage of miners' terraces have been preserved and refaced in the original red brick. No Jack and Vera Duckworth stone cladding, mercifully.

More than enough of the families who lived in these terraces over the past century or so suffered terrible personal tragedies at various times. As recently as 1979, ten miners were killed by an explosion at Golborne Colliery. At nearby Abram, 75 men died in the Maypole Colliery disaster of 1908. Two years later, on 21 December 1910, an incredible 344 men and boys perished at the Hulton Colliery, known locally as the Pretoria Pit. 'I was born in Atherton, where a lot of them came from,' Alan explains, 'and as kids we used to play on the site, not really understanding that beneath our feet was the scene of the third biggest disaster in British mining history.'

He's telling me this as we've passed through Abram and turned left towards Leigh. The site of the Parsonage Colliery was smack in the town centre. On a Saturday afternoon its wheel would have provided a distinctive backdrop to a rugby league match in the foreground. There's nothing distinctive about the site now. It houses one of those soulless retail parks that could be anywhere in the country. Leigh RFC plays its rugby elsewhere and the colliery was closed in 1992 along with Golborne and Bickershaw. Just under twenty years previously they had all been linked underground in the era of the so-called

closed five years ago. The Orwell pub looks as though it's still open, however, not far from the reference library. 'He signed the visitors' book there under his real name of Eric Blair,' says Alan, who ought to know about these things. He used to be the Wigan Borough archivist after leaving the pits, as well as the curator of the Lancashire Mining Museum. Not to mention being the author of half a dozen books on mining, including one called simply *The Wigan Coalfield*.

We're on our way to have a look at what has become of that coalfield in his vintage BMW. But on the way from the station to the car park, he has been telling me about the way that Wiganers in the town centre would dig up their back yards in search of coal. We're talking about the 1800s now. On his mother's side at least, Alan can trace his mining heritage back to the early part of the century before last. 'I think it was my uncles' stories about life underground that made me want to be a miner,' he muses. 'My attitude has always been that life is one 'superpit' when demand for coal had seemed limitless. The national strike of 1972 had brought home to householders and businesses their dependency on the stuff to keep the lights on and the wheels of industry turning – a point that Orwell had made so powerfully in 1937.

Parsonage, incidentally, had been one of the deepest collieries in the country and therefore one of the hottest. Men working at the face had to remove their footwear (clogs pre-war; standard-issue Coal Board boots after 1947) to pour out the sweat.

And so to Bickershaw, once the hub of a seven-mile network of underground conveyor belts. We get out of the car to peer through the long, high fence now encircling Alan's former workplace. Slowly but surely the landscape is being remoulded. On the other side of the road the former slagheaps look more like prehistoric burial mounds. 'They were twice as high when the pit was working,' he assures me.

It's a freezing cold day and, across a post-industrial wasteland pitted with iced-over puddles, we can see trees on the horizon with the tops of a few canal boats just visible beneath them. 'I think there's going to be some kind of marina over there.' Alan's hunch is confirmed when we walk to the far end of the fencing and find what appears to be a brand-new swing bridge providing access to barges one way and road traffic the other. Gulls are landing and then skidding on a frozen lake beneath which was one of five shafts. Looking across the lake and back to the wasteland, we can see a thin pipe issuing methane from the abandoned workings below.

Beyond the new swing bridge, the land seems to fall away quite sharply. 'Subsidence,' Alan declares. 'That's what created Pennington Flash beyond the trees. It's been a nature reserve for many years now. Some twenty-six feet of coal in total was extracted from various seams beneath this area from the late 1860s onwards. When I worked here, we were passing by at almost three thousand feet below the surface.'

Now you might imagine that he wouldn't really miss the heat, the discomfort and the back-breaking hard work at the coalface. But *au contraire*, as they rarely say in Wigan. 'From the start I felt proud to be part of the ancient tradition of British mining and the harder it got, the more I enjoyed it,' he maintains. 'You were on your knees and yes it was tough work, but it was a challenge. There was also a good camaraderie at Bickershaw, where a lot of the miners were local men. There were three pubs nearby and we'd all go for a pint after work.'

Quite a few pints, it would seem, to put back some of the weight lost through sweat. But what did the men make of someone like Alan? Did they know about his O levels and A levels?

'I used to keep quiet about my education. The humour down the pit was merciless and they'd really have laid into me. Also, I didn't want them to think I was showing off.'

Bryn Hall closed ten years before Alan was born and he's not sure of the exact location. But we know we're getting close when we reach the no-man's land between Bamfurlong and Ashton-in-Makerfield and pass a pub called . . . well, the Bryn Hall. It's closed. But the owner of the shop over the road leans on a jar of Uncle Joe's Mint Balls, another local delicacy, scratches his head and suggests that we try down nearby Bryn Gates Lane.

It sounds feasible but turns out to be wrong. We eventually locate the site on the other side of the main Bolton Road. It's about half a mile up a winding track between sparse and scrubby fields just beyond another row of miners' cottages. One of several dog walkers hereabouts is adamant. He's a Scot of venerable vintage who assures us that he's talked to the 'old-timers' and they've all confirmed it.

Alan nods sagely. The trees that have been planted here are in the formation

Women sitting on coal during a Wigan mine strike.

typical of a former colliery site, he suggests. 'There'll be a capped shaft in there somewhere.' He also points to the slight ochre-coloured tinge to the water in a nearby stream. Typical seepage from colliery waste apparently.

Mission accomplished then. I've finally paid my respects to the spot beneath which Orwell gathered the material to write such an inspirational piece of first-hand reportage. As we walk back to the bottom of the track, I can't help wondering what he would have made of the modern house on the other side of the road with an England flag flying in the garden. Well, despite his democratic socialist credentials, he was a patriot. In an essay called *The Lion and the Unicorn* he waxed lyrical about English culture and came up with a line about 'old maids hiking to Holy Communion through the mists of the autumn morning' that John Major's speech-writers would tap into many years later. In *The Road to Wigan Pier*, however, he was trying to make one part of England

A couple walk towards Parsonage Colliery in 1980.

aware of the plight and the contribution of the other. Nearly eighty years on, we no longer rely on coal alone to provide heat and light for our homes and power for our industries. But that doesn't stop the final paragraph of chapter two being a moving piece of prose that said much about the times in which it was written:

It is only because miners sweat their guts out that superior persons can remain superior. You and I and the editor of the *Times Lit Supp*, and the poets and the Archbishop of Canterbury and Comrade X, author of *Marxism for Infants* – all of us really owe the comparative decency of our lives to poor drudges underground, blackened to the eyes, with their throats full of coal dust, driving their shovels forward with arms and belly muscles of steel.

POSTSCRIPT:

Local journalist Geoffrey Shryhane kindly put an appeal in his column in the *Wigan Observer* asking if any readers had worked at Bryn Hall. It was more in hope than expectation on my part, the pit having closed so long ago. But a few days after my return from Wigan, I took a call from one Norman Prior, sounding remarkably robust for a man of ninety-four.

He lived at Croft Cottages, Bryn Hall, left school at fourteen in 1933 and joined his father and brothers at the colliery the following year. He trained as a fitter, working on the surface as well as underground where he might be called upon at any time of the day or night to fix the conveyor belt or coal-cutting machines, among other things. 'You didn't always know who the visitors were and I wouldn't have recognised Orwell,' he told me.

Norman's work proved good training for what was to come when he joined the Lancashire Fusiliers in 1939. 'I remember once being partially buried when a shot-firer shouted a belated warning and we had to dive for cover,' he added, almost chuckling at the memory.

By 1940 he was up to his chest in water rather than coal. Despite being a non-swimmer, he was just off the beaches of Dunkirk pushing heavily loaded rowing boats out to sea. Eventually he was picked up by a minesweeper and made it back to Blighty where he retrained as a tank driver and gunner. He then fought his way through North Africa and Italy before arriving in Palestine in time for the uprising.

When he finally made it back to Bryn Hall, the job he had been promised on his return had gone. The pit had closed. Disappointed but undeterred, he took a job with an engineering company on the outskirts of Manchester and finished up as works and production director.

So this has been the story of three remarkable men: George Orwell, an Old Etonian who took the road to Wigan Pier; Alan Davies, grammar school boy who chose to work as a coal miner; and Norman Prior, who had an elementary education, followed in his father's coal-dusted footsteps, yet eventually became a company director – but only after prolonged exposure to the university of life above ground.

CARRS, NENTHEAD

MY OLD BOOTS ARE about to have their first outing since they were overwhelmed and squelchily awash as they waded through knee-high water in Devon's last iron mine (see Great Rock, page 27). That was on a considerably warmer day than it is today, so it's a relief to ease in the toes tentatively and discover that the insides have finally dried out. These boots were made for hiking and, in other circumstances, it would be bracingly diverting to be tramping over the stunning countryside here on the east side of Cumbria, one of the most rugged sections of the Pennine Way.

Instead we're going down a long-disused lead mine. Just as well, perhaps, as the hills are coated in snow. The main road through Alston, the highest market town in England, had been closed by a blizzard only two days previously. The nearby village of Nenthead is even higher and the old boots are soon crunching over frozen puddles half a mile or so from the Miners' Arms. Here on this rutted, cratered path, the landscape has taken on that scarred and decidedly post-industrial look that appealed to and inspired the great poet W.H. Auden, a regular visitor when there was still some industry here.

To the left are former mine buildings, including the blast furnaces where lead was smelted. Nearby are tips of waste rock that had to be separated from the lead ore by young boys, usually up to their armpits in freezing-cold water. Ahead is a rusting truck that used to pull ore out of the mine on what are now equally rusty tracks. Even the River Nent, gushing past to our right, has brownish deposits in it – though they are apparently more to do with the output of a nearby hydroelectric plant than with lead mining.

The mine itself was known as Carrs. 'Without an apostrophe,' I'm assured by my guide, former mining geologist Peter Jackson. 'Carr' was the local word for a crag and there are a lot of them round here.' Yes, that landscape is decidedly craggy and no doubt the same could have been said about the miners who used to work here. There were around 400 of them when Carrs closed in 1921. Lead mining in the UK was in steep decline by the early part of the twentieth century, undermined by cheaper imports from elsewhere. In the previous century, and indeed the one before that, this area had been riddled with lead mines. Killhope, just over the border into County Durham, closed around 1907 and is now a mining museum. Nentsbury, even closer to here, survived until just before the Second World War, but by that time only around forty men were still employed.

The last lead mine in the Lake District was Force Crag at the head of the Coledale Valley, not too far from Keswick. From the 1880s onwards, it kept closing down and reopening. By the 1930s mining companies were more interested in barite – used in everything from drilling fluids for oil and gas exploration to barium meals in hospitals – than in lead, which was increasingly seen as a by-product. Force Crag's most recent incarnation was from 1984 to 1990, when a large-scale collapse flooded the workings.

In other parts of the country lead mining had continued sporadically. Among the outposts were Halkyn in Flintshire, where it went on until the 1970s, Snailbeach in Shropshire (until 1955) and the Derbyshire Peak District (until the late 1940s). Unlike its equivalents in Derbyshire, Carrs was a typical north of England mine. Instead of solid limestone, it was lined by what Peter calls 'loose, shaley walls' providing comparatively easy access to deposits. 'What they'd do,' he says, 'is drive into the soft shale and come up at the bottom of the limestone where veins of lead and zinc were found in the faults.'

If that makes lead mining here sound comparatively comfortable, think again. Silicosis was rife in Nenthead and district. By the time this mine closed, compressed-air mechanical drills had been introduced but the water used to damp down the effects of the dust it produced had not. 'There were quite a few blind miners as well,' Peter points out. 'They were using black [gun] powder, having drilled a hole in the rock, and then tapping it in with an iron bar. Guess what happened? Eventually some bright spark – oh dear, not quite the right expression – came up with the idea of putting a bit of brass on the end to stop it sparking. Then they went to rammers made wholly of copper.'

There were other occupational hazards. The lead ore, or galena, wasn't poisonous in itself, but the smelting process gave off gases and particles that could have grave effects on the surrounding countryside and indeed on the blood of the workforce in the immediate vicinity. Just as well, you might think, that the mines hereabouts were owned by a hospital. Well, yes, except that it was sited well over 300 miles away. The manor of Alston Moor had been owned by James Radcliffe, the third Earl of Derwentwater, but, after his head had been parted from his shoulders as punishment for his part in the first Jacobite Rebellion of 1715, George I had granted the estate to the Royal Hospital for Seamen at Greenwich. 'It held on to its northern estates until 1963,' says Peter.

By now we're at the gateway to the mine and luckily he has the key. After all, he's chairman of the trust that reopened Carrs in 1998 and restored it as a tourist attraction. It closed again comparatively recently, the trust having run out of money, but the chairman seems more than happy to give me a personal guided tour. Duly kitted out, I follow him in and much of our subsequent conversation is carried out from a slightly crouched position with Peter a yard or two in front. The tunnels here are under 6 feet high. *Well* under in parts, I should say, as one who's 5ft 11in but has gained an extra inch with the helmet. Every now and then it impacts with the roof, issuing the sort of crack that makes me feel very grateful that my cranium is well protected.

My boots are providing more than adequate protection too. Unlike the iron mine in Devon, the floor here is on a slight slope, allowing any surplus water to flow out of the mine. So, although it's muddy in parts, we can walk rather than wade. Water drips on to the helmet at regular intervals. The light on the front illuminates the moisture on the timbering that supports the roof. Eventually it forms into large droplets laden with zinc deposits.

'Zinc used to be a by-product of lead mining in the nineteenth century,' Peter explains. 'But as the twentieth century moved on, the process was reversed. Zinc became the more valuable.' It still is. In this country lead is more likely to be nicked from church roofs rather than mined. But with the possibility of a world shortage of zinc, an Irish company called Minco has already started prospecting in Northumberland, County Durham and Cumbria.

Not here at the Carrs mine in Nenthead, mind you, where it's a relief to the neck muscles to find ourselves suddenly able to stand upright in a chamber at least 14ft high. This is one of the places where the miners would have driven upwards, pursuing veins of galena high into the limestone. There would be other minerals in there as well, apart from zinc. 'The reddish stain in the roof area is iron mineralisation,' Peter points out. And what about that dark, shiny stuff that looks a bit like chocolate sauce? 'That's manganese.' There's quartz, too, as well as fluorspar and traces of silver. 'Back in the nineteenth century,' he goes on, 'Lord Allendale of Northumberland was a renowned gambler on the London tables and, when he was out of cash, he'd bet on the sales of silver that he'd get from his lead mines.'

Smallcleugh Level Mine, Nenthe

We move on down another tunnel, supported not by timbers but by the work of men who built the many dry-stone walls that you still see all over the rural north of England. When the lead mines round here were going full tilt, trees were in short supply – partly because so many had been chopped down to make roof supports and partly because of the damaging effects of pollution from the smelting process. A lengthy flue had been constructed to disperse the fumes away from the village, only to lay waste to vegetation and wildlife out on the fells. Such was the skill of those dry-stone wallers, however, that the tunnel arch looks as solid now as it must have done when it was first completed in 1805.

Emerging in another, much bigger chamber, we can see the limestone scarred with orangey-red iron deposits. The silvery-grey galena, however, is noticeable by its absence. 'That's because it's been worked out,' says Peter. 'I've seen a record from the 1830s when this chamber was first discovered. The report suggests that the men couldn't believe their luck. It was like being in a huge room, filled with lead ore. And instead of the usual vertical veins, in here it was in horizontal seams as in a coal mine.'

It feels as though we've reached a cul-de-sac, the end of the mine. But no. We're going onwards and upwards apparently – up three flights of steps indeed to emerge into sudden daylight. The temperature drops again from the constant, though damp, eleven degrees underground to near freezing. Ahead a waterfall cascades down the hillside, but it's not half as pure as it looks. 'The Nent is one of the most polluted rivers in England,' Peter maintains. 'The Environment Agency is trying to find ways of clearing it up.' Apart from the brown stuff issued by the hydroelectric station, it's full of zinc that is still

Smallcleugh, Nenthead mine entrance, sometime before it closed.

leaching away from the disused mine. There may not have been a mine here at all had not men first spotted this gap in the hillside and followed it in. I ask Peter when that would have been.

'Well, they were certainly mining here by the mid-1600s.'

By the 1960s, when he was a student, there were still miners alive who had worked here. 'They were in their seventies by then and remained hopeful that the mine might reopen one day. Harold Wilson's government had funded some mining exploration work around here.'

Had anything come of it, conditions in the smelting plant would hopefully have been a little less poisonous than they had been in the 1860s and earlier. But it would be a mistake to imagine that the London Lead Company, which ran the mine on behalf of Greenwich Hospital, was part of the great tradition of the dastardly Victorian landlord. On the contrary. Compared to most of those running mines at the time, they were positively paternalistic, perhaps because there was a strong Quaker element among the management. Throughout the nineteenth century they laid on a series of welfare provisions and public works for the miners' families in Nenthead. A subscription fund was established as early as 1817 to cover sickness, accident and death, with provision for widows and children. And a public water supply was laid on in 1850 with public baths and a washhouse following in 1865. Meanwhile, there had been comparatively generous investment in educational facilities. New schools came in 1819 and 1864. The reading room installed by London Lead in 1833 was one of the first free libraries in England.

Consumption of alcohol went down to the point where pubs began to close. That may have had something to do with the influence of Quakers, itinerant Wesleyan preachers and the temperance movement. But Peter has another theory. 'The company was funding schools for free, encouraging people to go to further education and, in a few cases, on to university. I think more than a few of those miners became more interested in learning and less keen on drinking.'

Towards the end of the century, however, change was afoot. Exit LLC in 1882; enter the Vieille Montagne Company in 1896 and the revival of lead mining. As the name suggests, it was not an English company. It was Belgian. What's more, they brought in workers from all over Europe to work at Nenthead, including a fair sprinkling of Italians on very low wages. Cue unrest among the locals and a few violent disturbances. The appointment of a German under-manager in the build-up to the First World War went down like a . . . well, a lead balloon. Once the war was under way, however, the foreign workers were declared to be 'aliens' and were impelled to return home. The last ore was brought out within three years of the war coming to an end. Smelting continued on a small scale for a while as the spoil tips were reworked for discarded lead. And now the mine's revival as a tourist attraction has also ceased, for the time being at least.

All we can hear when we emerge from the gates is the gush of the River Nent as it rushes past down the hillside. I ease off my boots and we head west, relieved that no more snow has fallen. The road through Alston remains open. A low and blood-red orb sinks behind one of those white-peaked mountains. But if Minco find the zinc, oh, the sun may not yet have gone down completely on mining in this area.

'The best ore on the planet,'
according to former Egremont
miner Gary Connell.

FLORENCE, EGREMONT

THE MORNING AFTER emerging from the disused lead mine at Nenthead, it's westward ho once more across Cumbria to the last deep working iron ore mine in Europe. There was still some underground walk-in mining at the Florence Mine in Egremont until 2008, when the site also doubled as a heritage centre. Now there's neither mine nor museum. There is a pile of saleable ore in the yard, however, and the Egremont Mining Company still functions (just about) from an office that looks as though it has changed little since the deep-shaft mining ceased in 1980.

A pile of phone directories totters precariously on the edge of a shelf. Beneath it stand a discarded pair of wellies, liberally coated in red dust, and a tall waste-paper bin that is full to the brim. On the opposite wall of faded magnolia, peeling in parts, the Health and Safety Rules dangle slightly askew. Beneath their curled-up edges is a filing cabinet, the metal top of which has corroded as acids or salts seep from various chunks of mineral piled on top. There's a vintage whistling kettle on there as well and, incongruously, a bottle of Wash and Go shampoo. To the left of a solid central table is a desk on which stands what now seems like an ancient, far-from-flat computer screen shrouded in a faded red shawl.

'We had a secretary once and she used that thing,' says mining engineer Gilbert Finlinson, eyeing the computer suspiciously. 'I don't do emails. Or texts,' he adds. His must be the last business in England reliant on a landline (with no answer-phone) and a fax machine.

Gilbert is seventy-seven. He has just shaken hands with us in the sort of sawn-off woollen gloves once favoured by bus conductors. With me today is my old mate Mick Botterill, who is chauffeuring me around his adopted county. The previous night we stayed with him and his wife Liz at their home in Kirkby Stephen. We've just dropped our womenfolk off for a morning's shopping in Keswick before driving on through a landscape that looks spectacular in the sharp light of a magical winter's morning. Frosted fields and snowy mountain-tops are sparkling in a low sun that spills gold on the mirrored surface of the lakes.

But as we've travelled further west, the countryside has become slightly more mundane, the towns and villages more work-a-day. These terraced houses would have been occupied by miners and their families in the days when this whole area was riddled with iron mines. In the nineteenth and early twentieth centuries, there were between two and three hundred within twelve miles of Egremont. (Their legacy lives on. Homes had to be evacuated here in November 2012 after a drilling rig being used to cap a former mine with concrete fell into a shaft and opened up a crater 75 feet wide that encompassed eight back gardens.) Some of the mines were small-scale but still sources of employment. The coal measures were further west, towards the coast, as we shall see in the next chapter.

As a Black Countryman who grew up in Darlaston surrounded by factories and foundries, Mick wonders aloud about where the people who live in these houses earn a living now that there are no mines and very little industry. The Sellafield reprocessing site would seem to be the answer in some cases, although it's now in the hands of the Nuclear Decommissioning Authority.

It was a contract with Sellafield that gave the Florence Mine a lifeline. 'They needed water and we had plenty of it after the deep shaft shut and the mine flooded,' says Gilbert. 'They brought a portable generator, put pumps into the shafts and paid us £12,000 a month until about five years ago when they terminated the contract.'

So what keeps the Egremont Mining Company going now?

Who wants to buy from that great pile of ore in the yard?

'A Swedish company called Mileco,' says Gilbert, confirming Mick's suspicions that, if it's anything to do with mucky manufacturing, it would no longer be British. 'We sold them sixty tons a couple of months ago,' Gilbert goes on, before explaining: 'There are two basic products. One is annealing ore, ground down and used to extract carbon from castings. The other is really fine, like talcum powder, and used to make red pigments for bricks or lipstick or paint.'

A bit like the ochre from the iron mines in the Forest of Dean?

'No, this isn't soft like ochre. It takes a hell of a lot of drilling to get it so fine.'

He gets up and rummages around for a while, re-emerging with a large lump of reddish rock which he bangs down on the table with a resounding thud. Just picking it up again threatens to bring on a hernia. 'That's the best ore on the planet,' puts in Gilbert's colleague Gary Connell, who used to shovel the stuff for a living and maintains that he enjoyed it. Yes, really. 'Best part of my life,' he confirms. Even more fun, apparently, than the coal mine where he started working at fifteen nigh-on sixty years ago.

Whether you believe that or not, Gary's knows his stuff when it comes to the quality of the ore in these parts. The geological make-up of West Cumbria made it a prolific source of haematite. With its high iron content and marked lack of phosphorous, it was highly prized for the production of pig iron ideal for conversion into steel.

Mining on a significant scale began in the 1830s. There was plenty of demand, not least from the Black Country, but not enough local labour to cope with it by 1845. The date is significant as the first year of the potato

---

The yard outside Gilbert
Finlinson's office.

famine just across the water in Ireland. Not surprisingly, the ravenous Irish emigrated in some numbers. There was work on the west side of Cumbria and here were the men to do it – would-be miners to shovel out that haematite as well as navvies to sink more shafts and dig the railway embankments through which the processed ore would be transported away.

'There were still three stations in Frizington, when I grew up,' Gilbert recalls. 'It was like the Klondike round there at one time. "Little Ireland" they called it.'

By that time, of course, many of those with Irish ancestry would be second, third or fourth generation. But they still had their own distinctive culture and religion: Roman Catholic. Like the reddleman in Thomas Hardy's *Return of the Native*, they would be covered in red dust after work (albeit for different reasons) and have to walk home to have it washed off their clothes and skin. Quite a few of those pale-faced Irish Catholics must have felt uncomfortably like orange men at times.

When Gilbert started as an apprentice at the Beckermet Mine in 1952, everything ran on steam power. 'There were no showers in the changing room, just a horse trough with a steam pipe up the centre,' he says. 'It was a couple of years later when they changed the winding pump to electricity. Then we could get showered at work.'

Judging by his and Gary's chuckling reminiscences, there was evidently some tension in their youth between the indigenous natives of Cumbria and the sons and grandsons of immigrants from Ireland. There were some Scots, too. The pubs could be 'a bit lively' and 'if you went to the picture house, you had to go in a gang'. Gilbert smiles before adding, 'It's a lot mellower these days.'

Into that combustible post-war mix of mining families came more incomers from the poorer parts of Italy. And, like the American soldiers who had not long left these shores, the Italians had an allure that set female hormones aflame. 'There was obviously trouble when someone found out that his missus had been seeing an Eyetie, and they didn't much like their daughters marrying one,' says Gary. 'Mind you, there were no fights underground. You looked after each other down there. I loved it and I ended up learning a bit of Italian. They were good workers.' He smiles fondly at memories of distant days and suddenly remembers a colleague called Tucker Sanderson. 'Always singing he was. Everything echoed down there and, whatever level he was on, you could hear him all over the mine.'

So did any opera-loving Italian become Tucker's mucker?

'Not that I remember, but they got on OK with him. Everyone did.'

As with most miners, it's the comradeship and what the Irish would call the 'craic' that he likes to remember. The work itself must have been back-breakingly tough in difficult conditions. But at least there was no methane in

hard-rock mines such as this one. Unlike the gas-plagued coal miners of the Cumbrian coast, they could smoke at work.

By the time Gary had moved from coal to iron mining, the economics of the industry were beginning to change. Ore imports from mainland Europe were beginning to increase again. During the 1960s the local furnaces closed down, along with many independent mines. Florence and its sister mine at Ullcoats were the only independents to survive – for a while at least.

The first shaft had been sunk in 1914, just in time for Egremont's fine ore to make a contribution to the First World W-ore effort. Mrs Muir Ritchie, wife of the chairman of the Millom and Askam Haematite Iron Company, turned the first sod. She was affectionately known to him as Florence so, when it came to naming the mine, Florence it was.

Like almost everything else, iron mining was badly hit by the lengthy economic recession of the 1930s. It was also being undermined, as it were, by cheaper imports from Spain – until that benighted country's civil war at least. Then came the Second World War and everything was changed, changed utterly. Such was the demand for iron ore that Florence was beginning to be worked out. A second shaft had to be sunk in 1945.

Further fundamental change came twenty-three years later. On 22 March 1968, Harold Wilson's government passed the Iron and Steel Act, bringing 90 per cent of British steelmaking into public ownership. Millom and Askam were among the 10 per cent left in the private sector. 'They thought they were going to be frozen out of the market,' Gilbert reflects. 'So they went into voluntary liquidation.'

He shuffles off again and re-emerges with the sort of ledger that Bob Cratchit might have scratched away at with a quill pen. It's enormous and hits the table with almost as much force as that chunk of red ore. Gilbert doesn't so much as flick through the pages as lift them one by one, with the care of a librarian at the Bodleian, his arm going through a complete arc each time. Eventually he comes upon the entries for July 1968, when the workers were sent on holiday with three months' notice.

There is no mention of 13 September 1968, otherwise known as 'Black Friday'. But that, apparently, was the date when closure was confirmed. End of story?

Not by a long way. The following year the lease of Florence and Ullcoats was taken over by Gilbert's former employers at Beckermet. By now they were part of the British Steel Corporation and had the wherewithal to drive through and connect them all. By April 1970 there was a single mine stretching five miles from Calder Bridge to the Uldale Valley.

As we know, it lasted another ten years. By that time heavy industry was in terminal decline. Smelting stopped at the Workington Iron and Steel works as part of British Steel's rationalisation programme and that should have been the end for the mines that supplied them. But men like Gilbert don't give up easily. Along with a small number of former employees, he invested some of his redundancy money in setting up the Egremont Mining Company and used a lifetime of engineering skills to supervise the driving of a 175ft-long incline down a gradient of one in four.

That tunnel is now closed. We've just been out to have a look at the locked gates and cast an eye over that pile of ore in the yard. How long will it last? Your guess is as good as mine. What's more certain is that the return of deep-shaft mining here is about as likely as Gilbert opening a Twitter account or his company starting a Facebook page.

For Mick and me it's time to shake hands with the bus conductor's gloves again and continue our journey west to the point where Cumbria runs out and the Solway Firth corner of the Irish Sea sweeps in over miles of abandoned coal seams.

HAIG

What cataclysmic violence
Cast thee down so deep,
Who once was trunk and foliage
On plain and mountain steep?
What sent thee to thy sepulchre
Inanimate and still,
Encasing in thy volume
Such silent power to kill?

THAT'S THE FIRST VERSE of 'Coal Questioned (Its beginning, its demise)', one of many poems about mining in a collection of reflections by the late John W. Skelly (1913–2002). He began his working life loading tubs at the Wellington Pit, aged fourteen, and finished as under-manager at Haig Colliery, the last to close here at Whitehaven on the west coast of Cumbria.

Wellington and Haig: two famous commanders, separated by a century, who sent many men to their deaths. The collieries named after them were responsible for far too many deaths as well, considering that they were supposed to be places of work not warfare. Casualties along the Cumbrian coast had been plentiful ever since Saltom had become the first undersea colliery in England back in the early eighteenth century.

Every day men would set off for coalfaces up to five miles under the Solway Firth. What killed so many of them, however, was not the water above their heads but the methane gas that seeped into their nostrils and turned their tunnels and seams into potentially explosive traps.

Wellington led the grim toll. In 1910, an explosion took the lives of 137 employees, including seven members of one family and five of another. All those men had gone to work down a colliery shaft that was the most spectacular in Cumbria and probably the entire UK. It towered over the harbour in the form of a castle with a great keep, turrets and enormous crenellated walls.

An explosion at the nearby William Pit killed 104 men in 1947, just after nationalisation. As for Haig, here are the raw figures: thirty-nine died there on 5 September 1922; four more on 13 December 1927; fourteen on 12 February 1928; and twenty-seven on 29 January 1931. But that tells only part of the story. The fourteen who perished in 1928, for instance, were mining engineers and officials looking for the body of Harold Horrocks – the one still unaccounted for since the accident that had taken four men the previous December.

They had spent the whole of one Saturday in a fruitless search for him while also trying to ensure that the pit was made safe for the 1,100 men who had been idle ever

Relatives outside Whitehaven Pit, waiting for news of their loved-ones from the rescue team after the mining disaster, September 1922.

since he and his colleagues had been killed. Just before midnight, three explosions happened within fifteen minutes with enough force to send the engineers and officials flying. The workings filled with foul air. Eleven survivors managed to grope their way nearly three miles in pitch-darkness to the pit bottom. Almost immediately another rescue party was despatched, but their way was barred by the debris of widespread roof falls. Those fourteen bodies remain entombed there. They have never been recovered.

In the circumstances, it's a wonder that so many men were prepared to take the risk of coal mining in Cumbria. They did, of course, because there would have been little work elsewhere in the period between the

First World War, when mining began at Haig, and the beginning of the Second World War. At its peak the pit employed some 1,800 men; not to mention any number of 'screen lasses', as the women were known who worked all hours in miserable conditions sifting the quality coal from waste rock.

By 1939 the grim eighteenth-century Newhouses tenements in Whitehaven, where so many mining families had lived, had finally been replaced by new estates clinging to the cliff side. Today the roads and cul-de-sacs of grey social housing make a marked contrast with the stunning setting of what is now the Haig Colliery Museum. The former engine hall and winding-head gear have been lovingly restored and the wheel almost gleams in the bright winter sunshine that also sparkles on the surface of the sea just a few hundred yards beyond.

'It must have been reassuring to emerge from the darkness and take in that sea view on a fine day such as this,' I suggest to former face-worker Tom Norman, who quickly disillusions me by pointing out, 'There were a lot more buildings when the pit was open. You were bricked in on all sides, so you couldn't see the sea when you came up from the pit bottom.'

Tom started working here when he was fifteen in 1962. By that time there were more jobs elsewhere, not least at the Sellafield nuclear plant just down the coast. He had good cause to be wary of mining at Haig. Apart from anything else, his father's back

Above left: Number five shaft, at the pit top.

Above: Haig Colliery spoiling the sea view, 1971.

Right: An organised retirement photograph in the early 1960s.

had been broken by a roof fall. 'But I just fancied it down the pit,' he shrugs. 'And, to be honest, I enjoyed my time there and didn't suffer anything more than a split finger. You didn't think about the gas, or the sea over your head. You just got on with your work and your workmates. The camaraderie there was better than anywhere I've worked since. You'd see blokes thumping one another outside the pub on a Saturday night and working happily together on the Monday morning.'

He's telling me this in the welcome warmth of the museum curator's office. Pamela Telford describes herself as 'just a local', perhaps playing down her role in helping to preserve the heritage of the Cumbrian coalfield and her own family. 'My grandfather was a miner,' she confirms. 'Geordie Clements was his name and I was petrified of him as a child. He always had black rings around his eyes and he shouted a lot.'

So what brought to an end the mining tradition that had been threaded through families such as Pamela's for generations?

Economics, pure and simple. The Cumbrian coastal mines were not only plagued by gas; they were also riddled with faults. Haig was the last to go in 1986. It had lost £27 million over the previous ten years. 'The last five hundred and sixty men working here had been on three months' notice even before the [national] strike began in 1984,' says Tom who had once been part of a workforce of sixteen hundred. 'By the end there were a hundred and sixty-seven left on what was supposed to be

A day by the beach next to the remains of Wellington Colliery.

"development work". For all the difference it made, they might as well have been at home.'

Tom himself had seen the writing on the coalface a few years before the axe fell and had taken a job as a hospital porter on half the wages he was used to. 'I stuck it for three months and then went on contract work at Sellafield,' he recalls. 'It was like being at playschool. Once you'd got the job done, you had to wait for the foreman to tell you what to do next. Down the pit we'd just got on with it.'

And once you'd finished your shift, you got on with the rest of your life – breeding racing pigeons or whippets in some cases; growing giant leeks or marrows in others. John Skelly, as we know, wrote poetry in his spare time. Another former Haig miner, Paul Schofield, painted pictures of life at the pit good enough to be used for calendars and Christmas cards. Neither pitman painter nor pitman poet had been the beneficiaries of anything beyond rudimentary education.

Haig Colliery also produced rugby league players a-plenty. Substitute prop forwards for fast bowlers and the old cliché about 'whistling down a pit shaft' held true in Whitehaven. The town's team benefited greatly from mine-hardened men such as Eddie Bowman, Phil Kitchin, John 'Spanky' McFarlane and Arnold 'Boxer' Walker. Then there was Bill McAlone, who put in forty-five years at the pit as well as scoring twenty-three tries for 'Haven', as the club was known. 'On a Saturday they'd go down the pit at six o'clock, come up at twelve-fifteen and be ready for the kickoff at three,' Tom reminds me.

In those days, rugby league and rugby union belonged to two very different worlds, in England at least. Twickenham would have seemed even further away from Whitehaven than it does today, I can't help reflecting as we bid farewell to the mining museum and catch sight of a set of rugby posts starkly outlined on the cliff top. And the day after I – finally – make it home, I come across another poem by John Skelly, written to mark the final closure of the mine where he worked for exactly half of his eighty-eight years. 'The death of a pit, the pit of death' is the first line. Sadly, it could have been written about more than one of the collieries along this beautiful yet brutal coastal strip, this isolated outpost of the British coalfield on the northern edge of the Irish Sea. They all had the 'silent power to kill'.

Midlothian drama society
re-enacting life underground.

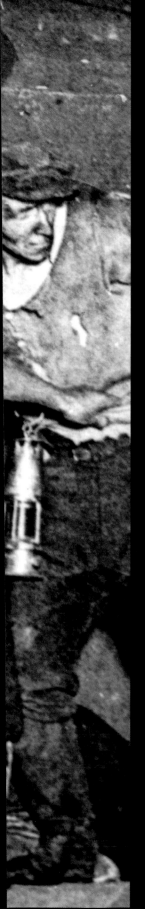

LADY VICTORIA

THE SO-CALLED 'PARROT' SEAM at Lady Victoria Colliery in Midlothian was not the hottest spot in a Scottish mine, but it was a little on the warm side. The temperature in some of the side roads was 85 degrees and the humidity was pushing 90 per cent. But the name had nothing to do with colourful birdlife from tropical climates. Parrot was a type of coal, soft and waxy and rich in gas and oil. It tended to make a loud cackling noise, like a parrot, when a match was applied to it. But it was also known as 'cannel' coal by James 'Paraffin' Young, who used to extract mineral oils from it at his Bathgate works in West Lothian before he switched to shale oil in the 1860s (see next chapter).

Many a miner here at 'the Lady' would emerge from this, the deepest seam, with parrot not so much on his shoulder as under it, hidden from the sight of officialdom. It was combustible stuff, by all accounts. One lump was guaranteed to set the hearth ablaze in seconds, sometimes with unpredictable consequences. 'You had to put the guard up because it really sparked,' says my guide Tom Young. 'My father was reading the *Edinburgh Evening News* in front of the fire when he smelled something burning in what he thought was the kitchen. It turned out to be a bit closer than that. A piece of parrot had spat at his newspaper and set it on fire. Luckily, he noticed in time and managed to stuff it back in the grate.'

Tom grew up in nearby Newtongrange, once the biggest mining village in Scotland and now a small town known for its annual brass band festival. He was born two doors away from the Dean Tavern, run under the so-called Gothenburg system whereby the profits are used for the benefit of the local community. He came from mining stock and grew up playing football with and against boys who would become miners. But he was not a miner himself. Instead he became a mining surveyor and started work at Lady Victoria in 1964. 'Although I'd grown up with the lads who worked here, I was still rocked back on my heels a bit by the very first shift I did,' he confesses. 'Until then I'd never realised the way that miners spoke to each other while underground. If they'd said those things on the surface, punches would have been exchanged.'

But surely they depended on one another and had to keep an eye out for each other? 'Oh, aye.'

And surely a tough job sometimes demanded a dry sense of humour? 'Oh, aye, very dry.'

He goes on to tell me about a character called Arthur Higgs, one of only two black miners in the area. 'He was a big feller, five-foot-ten tall and five-foot-ten wide. Arthur was very popular and they were always winding him up. He used to work with Jock the brusher [the man who maintained the underground roadways] and I remember watching them exchange swigs of water at the end of a shift. Suddenly they were in each other's faces, calling each other a black this and a white that. Then they burst out laughing, slapped each other on the back and climbed in the bogeys [the man-carrying trucks] together.'

Before he started at the colliery, Tom had been warned by an older surveyor that he would have to stand his ground with the miners or his life would be hell. After all, he had started work at eighteen rather than fifteen and had academic qualifications. Very suspect. 'This older guy told me: "If you're going to be an official down the pit, the miners will either think that you're a hard bastard or a stupid one. There's no middle ground." I thought about that when I was setting up my equipment one day and someone walked past and kicked my tripod. I took it to be an accident, but then he did it a second and a third time. Let's just say we had an exchange of opinions nose to nose. He said they had work to do and I told him there wouldn't be any work if I wasn't able to tell them which way to go. I also told him that my granddad could put up [roof-support] girders quicker and better than him.'

This frank conversation was evidently punctuated by a fair bit of effing and blinding. 'Oh, aye. You had to get down to the vernacular.'

The necessarily strict ban on smoking could have helped to make tempers a little shorter than they might have been on the surface. 'When the miners came up in the cage, the first thing the vast majority did was light up,' Tom recalls. 'A lot of them had cigarette packets hidden away all around the pithead. They'd managed to get through at least two fags on the way to the baths and I saw one or two trying to smoke in the shower with head back to avoid the spray.'

Below: Pithead buildings at Lady Victoria Colliery, 1980s.

Before washing away the coal dust, the men would hang up their soaking work clothes in the lockers provided. 'It was so hot in there that they'd be dry in two or three hours,' Tom goes on. 'I used to have three pairs of cotton socks which I'd peel off and put in the locker. When I pulled them out the next day, they were standing on end. I had to bang them on the concrete floor to loosen them up a bit.'

The pithead baths here at Lady Victoria were installed in 1954 and for the next thirteen years they were shared with the seven hundred or so men who worked at Lingerwood Colliery, just across the main road. Lingerwood closed in 1967. The two pits were linked underground and both were connected to Monktonhall and Bilston Glen, which became notorious for picket-line confrontations during the year-long miners' strike that started in 1984.

That was the year that Lady Victoria opened as the National Mining Museum of Scotland, having been shut down as a working colliery three years previously. The man charged with administering the last rites was George Archibald, chief surveyor for the whole of Scotland between 1981 and 1986, and it was evidently not a task that he undertook with any relish. 'Unfortunately, it was worked out,' he says sadly. That had been a familiar story north of the border for generations. 'There have been over 20,000 mines in Scotland at one time or another, and that's from records dating back only as far as 1872,' he goes on. 'Now there are no deep mines left at all.'

The central belt of Scotland, it seems, was spread

across a vast girth of coal. Pits abounded in Fife, the Lothians and Stirling as well as Lanarkshire and Ayrshire – the two counties that produced three of the most remarkable football managers that Britain has ever known. Matt Busby, Bill Shankly and Jock Stein all came from pit villages and were miners in their youth.

Busby was born in 1909 at Orbiston, near Bellshill, a place with just thirty-two cottages. Reflecting on his upbringing many years later, he said, 'There were only two ways for boys to go in those days – down, working in the pits, or up if you happened to be good at football.'

Shankly was well aware of that. He was born in 1913 at Glenbuck, anther tiny village close to the Ayrshire–Lanarkshire border, and worked at the local colliery. Not for long, however. He played for the Glenbuck Cherrypickers, a club that produced no fewer than forty-nine professional footballers between the 1870s and its demise in 1931. Shankly and his four brothers accounted for five of them.

Born at Burnbank, near Hamilton, in 1922, Stein worked at more than one local colliery while also turning out for Blantyre Victoria and Albion Rovers. He would go on to manage the Celtic side that became the first British team to win the European Cup.

What did these three men have in common?

Fierce determination and a competitiveness born out of desperation to escape. Also a reluctance to take orders from those who might consider themselves their social

Newton Grange Miners' Gala day.

superiors – directors of football clubs in other words. Busby took part in the General Strike of 1926 and remained a socialist for the rest of his life. A year before his untimely death in 1985, Stein was banging on the windows of a coach taking working miners through a picket line. Shankly built a team at Liverpool that played and worked for each other. Asked by a journalist what kind of player he was looking to buy, he replied, 'One who would shove a hutch [a coal tub] a hundred yards before he realised it was off the rails.'

These men were forged by the Scottish coalfield just as Sir Alex Ferguson, the man who eventually picked up where Busby left off at Old Trafford, was shaped by the shipyards of Govan. As Richard McBrearty of the Scottish Football Museum puts it, 'What they learned in those environments never left them.'

Back at the National Mining Museum, George is only too well aware of the debt of big-city football clubs to small mining villages in Scotland. 'This small country has

Above: Children swimming in the cooling pond at Loganlea Colliery, West Lothian.

always produced a lot of enterprising people,' he says. He's also aware that those small villages almost disappeared as collieries closed and the men moved on, taking their families with them. When Shankly's biographer visited Glenbuck in 1976, there were just twelve houses left.

The last deep mine of any significance to close in Scotland was at Longannet, to the north of the Firth of Forth. Really it was the remnants of several mines, established as recently as the 1960s and linked up underground to supply Longannet Power Station. The collieries of Bogside, Castlehill and Solsgirth were connected to Longannet to form what George calls 'a seven-mile mine with a double curve'.

He also calls its creation 'a major surveying job more complex than the Channel Tunnel'. He goes on: 'Luckily I had a man on my staff that I can only call a mathematical genius. His name was Young Robson – Young was his Christian name – and he'd started on the job before I took over. He lived in a caravan on site, which unfortunately cost him his marriage. When I became chief surveyor, Bogside was closing and he asked me if he could apply for early retirement. But we had one more connection to make – to Castlebridge – and I asked if he'd stay on. So he did and the connection was made. When I finally let him go, he was in his sixties and he died three months later. I always felt conscience-stricken about that.'

Castlebridge opened in 1984. It was the last deep coal mine sunk in Scotland and it lasted all of seventeen years. After it had been closed and filled in, the access to the Longannet complex was flooded in 2002. Luckily, the fifteen men working there at the time escaped unscathed. They were the last to come up from any depth in a Scottish coal mine. The end was nigh. It was not the end, however, of Scottish Coal's contract with the power station.

'We still had to find millions of tons from somewhere,' says Brian Murray, planning manager at the time. 'I remember sitting in the office discussing where we were going to bring it in from – Colombia, China or wherever – and looking out of the window. Within a few miles there was forty million tons of coal. But it's a matter of cost. There'll be no deep mining in Scotland again because nobody is going to invest millions to sink a shaft and only get a two-year contract. It was OK when there was a cosy relationship between two nationalised industries. Now everything's market-driven and there's no long-term planning.'

Today the power station uses imported coal as well as sources from Scotland's open-cast sector. One of the distinguishing characteristics of Scottish deep mines – seams of markedly differing heights at different levels – has been buried for ever. Lady Victoria had thirteen seams, ranging from over 8 feet to under 2 feet. As we continue our tour of his former workplace, Tom describes it as 'like a birthday cake with thirteen layers made from sponge three thousand feet high and five miles in diameter'.

That 3,000 ft seam, incidentally, was at Monktonhall. The Lady herself was only 1,650 ft deep. We're heading for the pit bottom now, using the stairs, which takes somewhat longer than it did for miners to descend in the cage, sixty at a time. They covered the distance in just eighty seconds and, halfway down, they were passed by sixty men coming up. 'Some visitors seem disappointed that they can't go down in a cage,' Tom confides. 'But they'd be terrified at that speed.'

The replica of a coal seam that has been created for visitors is one of the higher ones. In fact, the roof is well over my head. 'I worked in fourteen pits altogether,' says Tom, 'and for most of my working life in this industry I was crawling around rather than walking.'

Before nationalisation, the colliery was owned by the Lothian Coal Company, the property of whichever Lord Lothian happened to be alive at the time. In fact, the colliery was named after the wife of the ninth Marquis of Lothian, who was the first chairman of the company, formed in 1890. 'There was no set wage and miners would be paid only for the amount of coal that they could dig as individuals,' Tom goes on. 'If they were working in difficult conditions, the only way they could put food on the table was to work very long hours.' Then he pauses and points to a green hut. 'That was the weighbridge and what went on there was probably the start of the NUM [National Union of Mineworkers] up here. The man who sat inside worked for the coal company and knew which side his bread was buttered. "How do we know he's weighing it honestly?" the miners kept asking. They wanted their own representative in there to check and, eventually, Lord Lothian agreed. That would have been some time in the 1930s. By the 1970s people were saying that the NUM was becoming too militant, but by then it was easy to forget that these men had been downtrodden for generations.'

Not far from the weighbridge was the 'picking table' where 'old men, young boys and women of all ages' separated the wheat from the chaff or rather lumps of coal from other minerals that clung to it. The waste finished up on spoil tips or 'bings', as they were known up here. Maybe fragments of parrot or other combustible coal found their way in there as well because yellow smoke would sometimes issue from the pit banks, Tom remembers. 'If you had a young lady by the hand at the time it could look quite romantic with the setting sun behind it.'

The divine light of bings illuminated many another Scottish hot spot.

WESTWOOD

THE TAXI DRIVER conveying me away from Livingston North Station is not easy to understand. I haven't struggled with a Scottish accent so much since being approached by a Rangers supporter in Kennington tube station on my way to work, offered a 'wee dram' from his whisky bottle and invited to speculate on the result of the following day's match at Wembley Stadium in the days when England played Scotland on an annual basis. The taxi driver, I might add, is stone-cold sober. He's also friendly and helpful and seemingly intent on pointing out local landmarks.

By far the most prominent of these is the Five Sisters, a range of hills strung along the skyline like a knobbly knuckled clenched fist. There's oil in them there hills – or rather the search for oil was responsible for them being there in the first place. These are the spoil tips, or 'bings', for the last shale-oil mine in Scotland. Westwood closed in 1962, around the same time that Livingston was coming into being as one of the post-war new towns, built on the few square miles of land here in West Lothian that were not prone to subsidence because of mining. The site where the shale was processed is now covered by the Five Sisters Business Park, just outside the village of West Calder. Some of those passing by on the B7015 may be blissfully unaware of the dark and dirty past buried under those functional modern buildings surrounded by neatly marked car-parking spaces and, in some cases, well-trimmed lawns and bushes.

Just about every metal and mineral known to man has been mined in Scotland at one time or another. As well as coal, this neck of the woods had deposits of silver and iron ore. But the shale-oil industry dominated for almost exactly a century, from 1860 onwards. It was then that James 'Paraffin' Young, having exhausted supplies of so-called 'cannel' coal at his Bathgate works (five miles or so from here), switched to shale as a source of oil for his lamps and other patented products.

Initially from the east end of Glasgow, Young went to evening classes at the Andersonian College, where he made friendships and contacts with some of the cream of the Scottish scientific community. By the 1840s he was working as a chemical trouble-shooter in Manchester. After being sent a sample of oil from natural seepage at a mine in Derbyshire, he saw the chance to use a distillate to lubricate the looms of Lancashire cotton mills. Soon he was launched in a business partnership with one Edward Meldrum to produce and market the lubricant. But in 1848, supplies began to dry up. For Young it was time to look for other sources and potential products. Two years later he had taken out a patent for the production of paraffin, having identified Boghead, near Bathgate, as the best source of cannel coal and worked out the retorting process for extracting oil from it – a process that he adapted to shale just over a decade later.

The Five Sisters has been recognised as a structure of national importance by no less a body than the Royal Commission on the Ancient and Historical Monuments of Scotland, perhaps as a tribute to Young's inventiveness or, more likely, to the many thousands of men who once worked in the shale-oil industry. At its height, in 1912, there

Miners clearing up the working face after a shot has been fired c.1929.

were over 12,000 employees and output amounted to around 2 per cent of the world's oil production.

Decline began soon afterwards and it's something of a miracle that the industry survived for another fifty years. During the First World War, government-supported schemes to develop British interests in the Persian Gulf led to the beginning of the import of cheap crude oil. The cost of extracting oil at a rate of twenty-four gallons for each ton of shale meant the mines were eventually unable to compete with large tankers from the Middle East. Thereafter, as in so many fields of science, the export of expertise was Scotland's main contribution.

As you may have gathered, this information did not come from the taxi driver. Some came from Jim Henry, a former geologist and now a volunteer at the National Mining Museum of Scotland. Much more came from the excellent website of the Museum of the Scottish Shale Oil Industry.

The museum itself is part of the Almond Valley Heritage Centre, where the taxi drops me at the end of a five-hour journey involving three trains. The director, Dr Robin Chesters, speaks impeccable English in an English accent, and is a mine of information on this subject, so to speak. But he gives the impression that he'd rather I paid my entrance fee and wandered round the exhibition. Eventually I do just that, but not before he has put one or two things in context.

The cannel coal originally used by 'Paraffin' Young to extract oil was particularly soft and gaseous. 'Shale was altogether a tougher and denser rock,' he points out. 'It was brought to the surface and put into crushers that broke it down into lumps around the size of a man's hand.' And then? 'It was gradually heated, causing a vapour to be created – a mixture of waterborne chemicals and crude oil.' Even a dunce like me knows

that water and oil don't mix and it was easy enough to separate the two.

Some of the waterborne by-products, it seems, were more valuable than the oil before the First World War. 'Ammonia was used for fertilisers and explosives,' Dr Chesters explains. Three decades later, other by-products were used to create a multipurpose detergent. By that time, however, the use of shale to create oil was in sharp decline because of those imports from the Middle East and, indeed, the USA. So how did Scottish shale-oil mining survive until the early 1960s?

'In 1926 there was a commission of enquiry into miners' wages,' he reminds me. 'Even union leaders accepted that there could never be a commercial case for shale mining again. However, that would have put ten thousand or so people out of work and in places like West Lothian there were few alternative sources of employment. There would have been terrible hardship and perhaps civil unrest.'

So in 1929 a preferential rate of tax on home-produced road fuels was introduced. Two years later there was investment in new technology. A new plant was constructed at Pumpherston refinery to convert most of the industry's output into diesel and petrol. Quite timely

A group of refinery workers standing outside the air raid shelter at Westwood Oil Works in 1943.

as it turned out. Within a few years another world war was imminent and fears grew that external supplies might be cut off. A more efficient shale-oil works was built next to the established mine at Westwood in 1941.

Tom McVicar would have remembered it well. His father, Thomas Brown McVicar, was underground manager at Westwood Pit and his paternal grandfather was killed in a roof fall at another shale mine. 'Because of the nature of the seams, shale mining was inherently safer than coal mining as there was less chance of firedamp (methane),' Tom suggests. 'But it was more unstable than coal, leading to more cave-ins.'

Young Tom, as he then was, started working life at the 'topside' of Westwood in the 1950s. He soon moved indoors to take a job as office boy in the Westwood works. Over the next few years he rose to the 'dizzy heights' of wages clerk. He is now a Canadian citizen and has evidently been reflecting on his deep roots in the shale-oil industry judging by the lengthy article that he posted on the museum's website in August 2012.

Like many another, his maternal grandfather emigrated from Ireland to Scotland during the potato famine of the late 1870s and eventually settled in West Calder. Tom's mother was born in the evocatively named Happy Land, one of quite a few villages built by James Young's Paraffin Light and Mineral Oil Company to accommodate shale-oil workers. 'Even in the 1940s, which is the earliest I can remember, the rows of houses were basic,' he writes:

But they provided shelter, a place to start a family – in my case that would be my two older sisters and I.

We had a single electric light in each room, but no plug points. There was a toilet ('skunky') but no bath. The bath was a portable zinc one that we hung out in the garden until it was bath time. That meant every day for my father, who came home after a hard day's graft exhausted and sometimes unrecognisable under the dirt. The bath would be brought in, placed in the middle of the floor and filled up with water heated in pots and pans on the range. The scullery had a single cold water tap.

Most of the villages were razed after the pits closed down. But at one point there were over a hundred mines operating in the sixty square miles that delineated the shale fields, Tom points out.

In the 1950s, there were three in the immediate neighbourhood – Westwood, Breich and Hermond . . . The pollution caused by these three pits was outside any modern frame of reference. The rivers didn't quite run red; they were black and yellow instead. Falling into the black burn [water] meant burning your clothes as attempting to clean them was a waste of energy. Falling into the yellow burn solved the cleaning problem; it dissolved your clothing as you wore it. The problem with the yellow burn was trying to get out of your clothing before your flesh was eaten away. The confluence of both burns was a no-go area. Nothing lived there, not even weeds.

The bings, too, harboured hidden perils. 'If the bing consisted of greyish-black shale,' Tom recalls, 'it meant that the shale hadn't been retorted properly. There was still a large amount of oil locked up in there. This created the ideal environment for spontaneous combustion. At the old Gavieside works, near Polbeth, the bing flared up suddenly. The local story was that a cow wandered on to the top, unaware that it had been quietly smouldering under the surface. The poor bovine's weight caused it to break through the crust and . . .'

Result: instant roast beef, if a little overdone. Oxygen rushed in and there was an instant burst of flames. I find myself remembering that story as my taxi passes the Five Sisters on the way back to Livingston North Station. As far as I can tell through persistent drizzle, it's the right colour and, anyway, this quintuple-humped bing has been dormant for over fifty years. The cattle in this part of West Lothian can wander where they will and sheep may safely graze. It seems most unlikely that an ancient and historic monument of Scotland would spontaneously combust – and certainly not on a damp Monday afternoon.

Clocking In by Fred Laidler, 1948.
A Pitmen Painter.

ASHINGTON

ASHINGTON WAS ONCE KNOWN as 'the biggest mining village in the world'. The colliery named after it had six shafts alone and there were another four pits in the immediate vicinity. The horizon was dominated by winding wheels. Physically, that is. Metaphorically speaking, Ashington's horizons stretched far beyond the county of Northumberland. Or, to revert to a more appropriate metaphor, a dense seam of sporting, musical and artistic talent was unearthed from this coal-rich corner of the kingdom over several generations.

Only Jackie Milburn has a statue in the main street. 'Wor Jackie', of Newcastle United and England, is bringing a ball under control outside Burton's and looking as though he might be about to boot it through the window of H. Samuel. One day there may be another plinth under the likeness of Bobby Charlton, arguably the finest footballer that England ever produced. Bobby's brother Jack could be alongside him. Admittedly they haven't spent much of their later life in each other's company, but Jack was also part of the fabled side of 1966 that lifted the World Cup at Wembley. And he was sitting alongside Bobby in the Rolls-Royce that swept into their home town for a civic reception.

The town already boasts a pub named after the great West Indian batsman Rohan Kanhai, who spent a season here in 1964 and enabled Ashington Cricket Club to win the local league by finishing with an average of 93.62. Now Kanhai may have been 'a canny lad who liked a rum and a game of dominoes', as Harry Pearson records in *Slipless in Settle*, his wonderful book on northern club cricket; but, when all's said and done, he was just passing through. The Durham and England fast bowler Steve Harmison was born here. So too was the golfer Kenneth Ferrie, the Olympic rower Katherine Copeland and the operatic soprano Janice Cairns.

It goes on and it goes back, if we dig a little deeper into this rich seam. Art and theatre lovers will be well aware of the Ashington Group, recently celebrated by Lee Hall's play *The Pitmen Painters* – first at the Newcastle's Live Theatre, then at the National Theatre, no less, and finally on a national tour. It tells the story of how, in 1934, a group of Ashington miners invited the art lecturer Robert Lyon to teach them how to appreciate the works of Michelangelo and others. He visited their humble hut and, after a sticky introduction, managed to bridge a cultural gap wider than the Tyne. Soon they were producing their own paintings well enough to impress critics who knew what was what. But they still worked at the pit and their subjects emerged from their immediate surroundings – whippets, chip shops and, yes, other miners.

So how do we explain how a mining town of around 28,000, three miles from the Northeast coast and some distance from a significant urban centre, produced such a range of nationally acclaimed talents? Well, the Workers Education Association should be credited with introducing Lyon to the pitmen painters. As for football, it always has been seen as a way out for working-class lads; and they were as obsessed with the game in the coalfields of Northeast England as they were in the pit villages on the west side of Scotland. The Charltons' mother Cissie was a cousin of Jackie Milburn, while Jackie himself was one of five brothers who all turned professional. Ashington evidently had some shrewd judges of a 'good 'un' and they tipped off the scouts attached to top clubs at regular intervals.

Bill Ogilvie, now eighty-three, played in the same Ashington Hirst School team as Jimmy Adamson, who would go on to captain the Burnley side that won the league in 1960. As a young man, Bill remembers casting a judicious eye over a precocious kid playing for East Northumberland Schools on one of the miners' welfare pitches. 'He was younger and smaller than everyone else, but he stood out. Unbelievable ball control and so far advanced in technique. As for his shot, it was so powerful . . .' His voice trails away in a reverie of reminiscence. No prizes for guessing that he had just spotted the burgeoning talent of the boyish Bobby Charlton.

When he came back from National Service, Bill worked in the welfare office for the National Coal

'At one time Ashington had not only football and cricket pitches, but also a library and a theatre, several ballrooms and no fewer than five cinemas.'

Indeed the property developer Sir John Hall, another successful son of this town, has apparently maintained: 'I planned the Metro Centre in Gateshead to be the same as Ashington's main street where you could meet up with a neighbour, go shopping and then to a cinema. Ashington had the lot!'

Not any more. Facilities here are much diminished, as in so many towns that have lost their economic underpinning. One by one the local pits closed: Linton in 1968, Woodhorn in 1981, Ashington itself in 1988, Lynemouth in 1994 and Ellington as recently as 2005. Only two winding wheels remain, and they're attached to the Woodhorn Museum. As my bus from Newcastle rolls into town down Milburn Road and pulls up at the traffic lights outside what must be the biggest Poundland store in the world, I can see from the top deck that the horizon now is dominated by wind turbines. Presumably they're part of what passes for an energy policy in a country

Board in Ashington. It was his job to organise sporting and recreational activities between collieries. He'd done something similar before his call-up, but in those days it was for the Ashington Coal Company.

Now you may be surprised to learn that a private mine owner had a welfare section at all. Mine owners were supposed to be ruthless exploiters whose only interest was profit. But the company here was comparatively enlightened, according to Deborah Moffat of the colliery museum at Woodhorn, one of four former pits clustered around the hub of Ashington. 'They were very good at promoting extra-curricular activities to make their employees more rounded human beings,' she says.

that has sold off its utilities to foreign-owned private companies and sealed millions of tons of coal under the surface of this island while importing increasing quantities of the stuff from Poland, Colombia and elsewhere.

Of course, it's easy for those of us who never had to work underground to become sentimental about an industry that took such a toll on the health – and in some cases the lives – of those who had little choice in the way of employment prospects. Certainly Milburn himself was in no mood for warm reminiscence when he joined the 340 or so miners who left Ashington Colliery for the last time some 25 years ago. 'If I had my way, there would be no deep mines,' he told the industrial editor of the

Newcastle Journal. 'It's an awful thing to send people down a pit. They are not fit for dogs to work in. I was fourteen when I first went down Ashington pit as a trainee fitter and, to be honest, I hated it every time I had to go underground. Imagine what years of breathing that coal dust in can do to your health.'

Sadly, Milburn was brought up at a time when the health hazards of smoking had hardly penetrated the national consciousness. He died of lung cancer at sixty-four. In his and Newcastle's hey-day, the early 50s, he'd been known to have had a fag during half-time while playing at Wembley.

The rather more humble Portland Park, home of Ashington FC until 2008, is buried under a branch of Asda. It stands opposite the bus station where Larry Routledge picks me up in his hatchback. A rum character is Larry: worked at Ashington Colliery from 1950, when he was fifteen, to 1986, when he took early retirement two years before the closure. 'My knees, lungs and back were all shot,' he says. By that time he'd been a colliery deputy for nearly twenty years, but he'd also done his time hewing coal from the face in seams no higher than 2 feet in places.

When he started, this pit alone employed 3,775 men – ten times more than when it closed. 'It was like a big village underground,' he recalls in a Northumberland accent that makes the average Geordie sound like a BBC newsreader. As with any closed community, the miners of Northumberland and Durham developed a distinctive way of communicating that makes it difficult for an outsider to tune in. 'Pitmatic' is the name coined for the dialect they spoke in, and I've already had a crash course by listening to the reminiscences of Jim Slaughter, one of Larry's former colleagues, on the Woodhorn Museum's website.

I now know, for instance, what 'dadding the pit clothes' meant. It meant bashing them on the wall of the house to get rid of the dust when the men came home from work. As you might imagine, this was a job for wives. As Jim's disembodied voice puts it: 'The women were that proud, they wouldn't let their men go to work unless their boots were polished, their pit hat was polished, even their knee-pads were polished. They didn't want anybody saying, "Oh, look at that sloven".'

Kneepads, incidentally, were better known as 'hoggers'. A pit pony was a 'cuddy' and a 'glennie' was a lamp for testing gas. Larry still has his up in the loft. Eventually we'll be going back to see it over high tea in the spick-and-span house that he shares with his hospitable wife Margaret. For now he's giving me a guided tour of Ashington and district, including a glimpse of his childhood home on Fourth Row. 'We lived at number fifty-eight and the Milburns were at forty-nine. In the middle of the road, between the rows, were the netties.'

'Netties?'

'Toilets.'

'Ah.'

In keeping with the comparatively enlightened attitudes of the Ashington Coal Company, the miners' houses here were more spacious than in other parts of the country. And although they were laid out in rows with the considerably more spacious colliery managers' homes in the First Row, there were other streets that were named as well as numbered – after Shakespearean characters, would you believe, most of them female.

There's a Portia Street, a Rosalind Street and an Ariel Street. The Charltons lived in Beatrice Street.

Unlike hers, their story could hardly be said to be much ado about nothing. Satellite dishes now cling in clusters to the sides of modernised terraces so that residents can have beamed into their homes the deeds of today's mainly foreign-born footballing superstars, who are paid wages beyond the wildest dreams of the finest footballer that England ever produced. As for Milburn, he was the superstar who travelled to St James' Park, Newcastle, from Ashington every day on the bus.

Larry's hatchback drives on up the road towards

Eleventh Row. What was once Tenth Row is now a sort
of outer ring road lined with retail names to be found
anywhere in the Western world – Lidl, Aldi, McDonald's
and so on. On the site of the former pit, meanwhile, is
the Wansbeck Business Park. A sign outside promises
'Fully licensed sites in a new environment for business in
Ashington'. Inside are landscaped grounds with a small
lake and what looks from a distance like a cross between
a pagoda and an old-fashioned bandstand. One of the
businesses is called Polar Krush which, I later discover,

Lamp room, last shift, Woodhorn
Colliery 1981.

is a supplier of iced slush drinks to children. Another is Culpitt, makers and decorators of cakes.

Needless to say, any company that provides employment is welcome in a place like this. Jobs for young men in particular are nowhere near as plentiful as they were when there was a coal pit rather than Culpitt on this site.

Back at the Routledge household, Margaret tells me about her and Larry's grandson. 'He's twenty-six now and working in a call centre,' she says. 'Went to university, mind you, and got a 2.1 in media studies. He wants to stay round here, but there's nothing doing. The main street is desolate when it's not market day. I can only think of one decent shop that's left. It used to be bustling when the pits were open. There was good money about.'

While she's telling me this, I'm nodding sympathetically between mouthfuls. Larry has urged me to 'get stuck in' to the impressive tea that his missus has laid on. If this is Ashington hospitality, it takes some beating. There are ham rolls with pease pudding, slices of bacon-and-egg pie and thickly buttered scones. 'Champion,' as they say round here. And it doesn't take long to steer the conversation from pease pudding to leeks.

Growing vegetables for show has been part of mining culture all over the country. For men who spent long hours of daylight underground, the allotment must have seemed like a little patch of paradise on a summer's evening. But in the coalfields of Northumberland and Durham, the leek has always had star billing. A top grower such as Neil Armstrong was as well known and revered in these parts as the astronaut of the same name. That name was a gift for local newspapers. One of Armstrong's prize-winning exhibits produced a headline proclaiming: 'ONE GIANT LEEK FOR MANKIND'.

Size has never been the only criterion but, by God, it matters. To quote Harry Pearson again, this time from a piece in the *Independent* back in 1999, 'there are two classes of leek: "blanch", which are the size of broadswords and judged on length, and "pot", which are made like bodybuilders and judged by girth.' Tales of men staying up all night before a show to protect their prize exhibits from sabotage have passed into local folklore.

'All the clubs round here had big leek shows with big prizes,' Margaret recalls. 'They could win washing machines and fridge-freezers at a time when not many houses had that kind of thing.' Larry remembers his dad growing leeks fed by copious quantities of 'sheep muck'. He also remembers being in a club at the end of a show

Opposite, top: Milburn scoring in the FA Cup Final at Wembley, 7th May 1955.

Opposite, middle: If Ashington pit ponies could talk it would be in 'pitmatic'.

Opposite, bottom: Like miners everywhere, those in Northumberland depended on one another.

Right: *Whippets* by George Blessed c.1939. The Pitmen Painters' subjects emerged from their immediate surroundings and included whippet racing.

when things got a bit lively. 'Someone uprooted a pot leek and threw it across the room. It hit a trumpeter from the Ashington Colliery Band in the chest and sent him flying.'

When I suggest that those giant leeks wouldn't have tasted too good, they both confirm that they made a lovely broth. 'They used to make big boilers full of the stuff on a Monday after staging the competition at the weekend. Not many men went down the pit on those Mondays,' Larry insists. And after assuring him and Margaret that I couldn't eat another thing, I calculate that I've just about got room for a pint. It's time to pay my respects to Rohan Kanhai. After all, he was a star member of the great West Indian touring side of 1963. Watching his distinctive hook shot and Gary Sobers' distinctive everything on my parents' 12-inch telly in glorious black-and-white turned me on to Test cricket.

The pub named after Kanhai is conveniently close to the bus station. It's also packed just after five on a Tuesday afternoon, perhaps because you can buy a pint here for the princely sum of £1.69. Yes, it's a Wetherspoon's house and, like most Wetherspoon's houses, it's decorated with photographs and potted biographies of those who've made a mark in the locality. Apart from Kanhai himself, there's a tribute to the Charlton brothers and, above a corner seat occupied by mature women chatting animatedly over tea and Cokes, 'The Ashington Flyer'.

Milburn, in other words. When he was flying down the wing for Newcastle, crowds of nigh-on 60,000 roared him on, many with lungs already scarred by coal dust as well as nicotine. He was 'Wor Jackie' because he was one of them. As I rush off to catch the X22, it's a humbling thought that this hour-long bus journey was the daily escape route for a man who provided such rich entertainment for so many while being paid not much more than twelve quid a week. Yes, 'Wor Jackie' wanted to escape from the pit – but never from the world's biggest mining village.

MONKWEARMOUTH

WHEN ED MILIBAND addressed the 128th Durham Miners' Gala last year (2012), he was the first leader of the Labour Party to do so for 23 years. 'At least he was man enough to come,' says Davey Hopper, general secretary of the Durham Miners' Association. A crowd of over a hundred thousand turned up. Only a handful of those present, however, would have been working miners in the few open-cast sites remaining in County Durham.

When Monkwearmouth in Sunderland closed shortly before Christmas in 1993, it was the last deep mine in an area once riddled with them. The Durham coalfield contributed a massive 58.7 million tons to the national output of 270 million tons a century ago when UK coal production peaked. By the time of nationalisation, there were still some 127 collieries in the county producing a total of around 24 million tons.

That was back in 1947, of course. By 1974, numbers employed were down to 25,000 at just 22 collieries. What had happened in the meantime? Well, alternative sources of fuel had started to be used for railways, shipping and electricity generation as well as domestic heating. At the same time, the Coal Board had invested in mechanisation and, inevitably, there was a certain amount of rationalisation after nationalisation. Predominantly the closures came on the west side of the county while production was increasingly concentrated on the large coastal collieries.

One of them was Monkwearmouth, better known to the miners simply as Wearmouth. West Durham men either migrated south, with 8,000 moving to Yorkshire under schemes grant-aided by the NCB, or commuted long distances to the east. Davey himself had a rather shorter journey to work. He was brought up in Sunderland in a house on the same street as the main shaft (there were four altogether) and worked at Wearmouth from 1958 until 1985. 'I used to walk twenty yards to the pithead and then travel another two or three miles from the pit bottom to the face,' he recalls. 'Later we were eight or nine miles out.'

One of the many faces in this huge, labyrinthine colliery was some distance under the North Sea. The miners travelled so far in little trains, known as 'man-riders', and walked the rest. 'There was a saying down the pit: "If you were walking, you weren't fighting",' says Davey, who goes on to describe his former workmates as 'the greatest men on Earth'.

And the job?

'That wasn't the greatest. It was tough and difficult work.' Deadly as well, in far too many cases. The website of the Durham Mining Museum carries a list of fatalities here that goes on for screen after screen. There are 279 names in all over a period of 163 years. Look a little closer and you notice that the vast majority of those deaths happened in the era that preceded nationalisation. 'The early coal owners murdered on a weekly basis,' proclaims Davey, a stalwart of the National Union of Miners.

By 1846 the Hutton seam at Wearmouth went down to a depth of over 1,700

Previous page: Durham Miners' Gala, 1974.

Left: Sunderland Coal Staithes and Monkwearmouth Colliery, on the estuary c.1970.

feet. That made it 'the deepest coal mine in the world', according to the museum. But they would have disputed that claim at Snowdown in Kent and at Hamstead Colliery on the outskirts of Birmingham.

Frank Forster worked at Wearmouth and Hamstead (see page 89) and what he remembers most is not the depth of the respective shafts but the difference in the heights of the seams. 'I'm only five-foot-four and some of the seams at Hamstead were way over my head,' he recalls. 'At Wearmouth the lowest was two-foot-six and the highest not much more than four feet.'

Thirty years after Frank moved south and just before the pit was 'mothballed', miners broke through to seams that were 9 feet high. No lack of coal then; just a lack of will at the top level to carry on mining it. A report commissioned by the Collieries Campaign Group in 1993 and sent to the Right Honourable Michael Heseltine MP failed to move the man who was both the President of the Board of Trade and Secretary of State for Industry.

The report pointed out that shutting the last pit so soon after the 'demonstrably premature closure of Wearside's shipyards' would devastate the local economy at a time of national recession. And, sure enough, it did. Apart from the redundancies visited on over a thousand miners, there was a knock-on effect on the supply industry. Male unemployment in the city rose above 20 per cent.

And now?

At time of writing it is still over 14 per cent, not far off twice the national average. Davey reckons that around 10 per cent of former Wearmouth men 'have survived rather well, but the majority are in low-paid work or on benefits'.

Those who can still afford to watch Sunderland FC at the Stadium of Light must sometimes look at the multi-millionaires striding around that immaculate turf and wonder if they realise that beneath their designer boots is what Frank calls 'a bloody big hole'.

What the miners used to call 'Black Road' – presumably because of the generations of coal-blackened men who trooped back along it in the days before pithead baths – now leads to the home ground of the Black Cats. They moved here from Roker Park four years after the closure of Wearmouth. I'm on my way there now in a car driven by Chris Hall, who worked at the colliery from 1968 until it closed. He was a fitter, maintaining the machinery underground and mending the chain belts on the coalface whenever they broke down. 'More often, the deputies would be standing over you while you worked,' he says. What about the miners? 'They were usually glad to have a break.'

These days he's secretary and treasurer of the Wearmouth Colliery Social Welfare Club. It's known locally as the Duck Inn, overlooking as it does a cricket pitch where Sunderland legend Len Shackleton turned out for the home side in the summer months. Shackleton, an outrageously gifted inside-left of the old school, was known as the Clown Prince of Football. In late middle age he could still perform his party trick of flicking a 50p piece off the toe of his shoe and straight into his top pocket. Not a bad cricketer either by all accounts. A medium-fast right-arm bowler and a useful batsman, he was good enough to be selected for Northumberland in the Minor Counties League on the strength of his exploits for Wearmouth.

He died three years after Sunderland's move away from Roker Park. What he made of his former club playing on top of Wearmouth Colliery is unrecorded, as far as I know. As Chris's car approaches the ground, we can see the white metalwork of the cantilever stand looming over the rooftops of the rows of former miners' houses.

We park close to what is still called the Colliery Tavern where former manager Bob Stokoe – 'The Man, The Messiah, The Moment' – is captured in bronze celebrating the unlikely victory over Leeds United in the 1973 FA Cup Final. 'On that corner opposite is where we used to stand on the picket line,' Chris confides. A member of the Durham mechanics branch of the NUM,

he stayed on strike throughout the bitter dispute of 1984–5. There's a telling contrast between the ecstatic Stokoe and the grim predicament of those men just over ten years after that fabled final.

There's no shortage of reminders of the past round here. The previous evening Sunderland have lost one-nil to near-neighbours Middlesbrough in whatever the League Cup is called these days and, as if to comment on the home side's performance, a large pile of police-horse manure remains on the forecourt. Nearby are two black pipes protruding from the paving. 'They're taking out any methane to save a build-up underground, but it's quite harmless up here,' Chris assures me. All the same, the pipes are hemmed in by large metal containers the shape of light bulbs. Well, it is the Stadium of Light, I suppose.

An eternal light burns in a huge Davy lamp on what was once 'Black Road'. It's a monument that 'stands as a permanent tribute to the memory of those men and their families who took part in traditional industries' it says here, and it's sponsored by Northern Electric and Gas.

There's more. Round the corner is a huge pit wheel, its red spokes seeming to intertwine with the white struts of that cantilever stand. More mundanely, a plastic beer glass is lodged against one of the huge metallic boulders being pushed up the steep river bank in sculptor Graeme Hopper's 'homage' to generations of miners, their 'social struggle and will to survive against the odds'.

On the opposite bank of the Wear is the depot of Liebherr Cranes UK, recent winners of a Queen's Award for Industry in recognition of growth in overseas earnings. There certainly isn't much scope for selling cranes around here any more – not since shipbuilding preceded mining on the road to oblivion. I'm reminded of another comment by Davey Hopper. 'When I was a kid,' he told me, 'you couldn't get on the river for industry. Now you can walk all the way along the bank with nothing much in the way. Some people would say that's progress. But it's progress without a thought about how the majority of people can earn a decent living.'

That's a conundrum that Ed Miliband may one day have to grapple with in earnest.

Left, top: The home of Sunderland FC, The Stadium of Light, built on what was Monkwearmouth Colliery.

Left, bottom: Sculptor Graeme Hopper's homage to generations of miners on the banks of the Wear, next to the Stadium of Light.

Fryston Colliery canteen, rather different from the Samuel Valentine Urban Food Hall c. 1930s.

FRYSTON

AS HE GREETS ME AT CASTLEFORD STATION, Harry Malkin looks more Left Bank than West Riding. He's sporting a pointed beard and a rather stylish tweed cap. It's the look of an artist – a successful one at that, and deservedly so. But the accent is still broad Yorkshire and the commitment to commemorate the considerable mining heritage of this area undimmed by the passage of time. 'Nobody else is going to do it,' he says as we set off towards the nearby village of Fryston where he worked underground from 1966, when he was fifteen, to 1985 when the colliery closed two days before Christmas and not yet a year after the end of the miners' strike.

He had been a fitter, maintaining and repairing heavy machinery in the cramped spaces of low seams. His father, also Harry, was a ripper who used those machines to tear coal from the face. 'Big Harry', as he was known at the pit, played a part in the development of the precocious artistic talents of 'Young Harry', as a piece I wrote for the *Guardian*'s arts pages back in 1998 made clear. It started:

•

Many an artist has drawn on his father's influence. Perhaps only Harry Malkin has drawn on his father's back. It was a broad back. 'As big as a barn door,' he recalls. Malkin senior was a miner who worked almost naked at the coal face. When he came home, he liked to lie full length in front of a coal fire (the fruits of his labours) with his shirt off. Young Harry, who was eight or nine at the time, would set to with his Biro. Cartoons first, then eagles, dragons and other exotic creatures were inscribed like temporary tattoos . . .

You may be wondering why he didn't use a drawing pad instead. Well, it seems that paper was as rare as leather-bound first editions in some mining villages in those days. I remember Harry telling me that he and his brother and sister, also good at art, were always fighting over scraps of discarded wallpaper. For him the pad came later. First he used to scribble caricatures to amuse the lads underground at 'snap-time'. He used Biro at first, then pencil. But it was the switch to charcoal that imbued his work with the depth and tone that best suited his subject matter.

By that time the pit had closed and he could finally stand back and try to put a meaning to the vivid memories he had of what he and his workmates had been doing in those low seams. He wouldn't be the first professional artist to emerge from such a background. Far from it. Collieries have a long tradition of producing what you might call miner-artists. The Ashington Group from the 1930s (see page 139) have been celebrated by the touring National Theatre production of Lee Hall's *The Pitmen Painters*. Less well known is the Spennymoor Settlement, which helped to develop the considerable talents of Norman Cornish and another Durham man, Tom McGuinness. Both have works that are part of the collection of the National Mining Museum of England, which recently put on an exhibition of pitmen painters.

Harry's first exhibition started in a café in Pontefract in 1986 – 'somewhere between the serving hatch and the gents' as he puts it. Yet somehow it finished up at the Royal Festival Hall where it ran for three months instead of the expected three weeks. Every picture was sold in the first week.

It should be said that it was not just the Harry Malkin show. The extraordinary photographs of Jack Hulme, a surface worker at Fryson who became the village barber, were displayed there as well. 'I'm world famous round here,' Jack was fond of saying. That was after his pictures of everyday village life – miners wearing braces over vests sitting on scrubbed front steps; girls with skirts tucked into knickers high-jumping over sticks on bricks – finished up being hung on some very expensive walls in London and elsewhere. By that time Jack was into his eighties. He'd been taking pictures for decades with a Leica camera and never thought much about showing them off.

So who can we thank for unearthing two such talents from one colliery?

Step forward Brian Lewis who, at the time, was running the now sadly defunct Yorkshire Art Circus. An accomplished artist himself, he recognised the quality of Harry's drawings and Jack's photographs immediately. 'I remember asking Jack if he had any negatives and he led me into a cluttered back room where there were about ten thousand of them, mainly bunged in an old tea chest,' Brian recalls with his customary chuckle.

But how did an exhibition in a Pontefract caff end up at the Festival Hall?

'That was down to Olive Fowler.' Who? 'She worked in Arthur Scargill's office and managed to get hold of someone in London who was interested enough to ask to see examples of Harry and Jack's work.'

Just before he died in 1990, Jack was apparently heard to remark: 'I feel a little bit sick of heart. I've been robbed of something I've always lived with.' He meant Fryston Colliery. Not only did he work there for a while; he also looked over it from his front room.

COAL PREPARATION PLANT

At least the house is still there. Between a drainpipe and a uPVC front door is a blue plaque pointing out that this was the home of a 'colliery worker, hairdresser and celebrated photographer'. Harry's Peugeot has just pulled up outside. Having paid our respects to Jack's plaque, we look out over what he might have in his viewfinder if he was able to peer through it today.

It's very different from the scene that I remember from my last visit in 1998. Instead of ponies grazing on greyish grass in the shadow of landscaped spoil heaps, there is a new village green, funded by English Partnerships as part of an ongoing regeneration project and designed by the American landscape architect Martha Schwartz. The green is threaded with pathways and low stone walls. There's a stone sculpture too, which looks like a giant finger pointing skyward, as well as the obligatory model of a pit winding wheel and some wrought-iron bollards by Antony Gormley no less.

It's all very tasteful and easy on the eye. What the green lacks is much in the way of life. Admittedly it's a Friday morning and the swings in the children's playground are stirred by nothing more than a stiff breeze. The kids are at school, albeit in another village. Harry sighs: 'The school here went long ago. So did the shops. This used to be a thriving village with a chip shop

Above: Fryston Colliery, 1930s.

Left & right: Two of Harry Malkin's paintings of life underground at Fryston.

and a chapel, a newsagent's, butcher and Co-op.'

It helped, of course, that almost a thousand miners might be coming and going on one shift or another. 'A lot of them lived here when I started in the sixties,' Harry recalls. Others came from Castleford or adjoining villages. The Malkins came from Airedale, about a mile away, and the young Harry made various attempts on the four-minute mile on those occasions when he woke up five minutes before the six o'clock buzzer signalled the start of his shift at ear-splitting volume. 'I could run a bit in those days,' he smiles. 'We had a greyhound and I used to try to keep up with it when it was my turn to take it out.'

The greyhound, rather than whippet, was the miners' dog of choice in these parts. 'There was a track at Pontefract where they used to run for clocks and cutlery,' he goes on. 'Ian Clayton [author and another product of the Yorkshire Art Circus] wrote a story about it. The track must have closed down in the late fifties or early sixties,' Harry adds as we gaze at one of his works – a greyhound sculpted in local stone under the bridge that has always provided the only access in and out of Fryston. The stone mural was chiselled into being using one of Jack Hulme's photographs from the late 1930s as the inspiration. Holding on to the dog is a character who was known locally as 'Clinker' Steele. Always in and out of jail apparently. He's leaning on a wall with the local butcher and a character called Les

Oxtably, who was fourteen at the time but looks a lot older, perhaps because he's flat-capped and mufflered. Teenage 'gear' was still a long way in the future when Jack took that shot.

Before we climb back into the Peugeot and set off to look at the latest Malkin monument, I ask Harry how he feels coming back here. 'Very mixed,' he admits. Part of him misses the bustle of Fryston and the 'crack' between the lads – the bleak humour of men working in hot, low seams about a mile underground. Harry stayed out through the full twelve months of the miners' strike in the fight to keep the pits open. He knew full well that there would be few alternative sources of employment in an area like this that would pay a living wage. 'A lot of it's security work; fifty bob and bring your own dog.' On the other hand . . .

'I wouldn't want to go back. Not a chance. My dad retired through ill-health at sixty-two, the age I am now. He had pneumoconiosis [dust on the lungs], whereas my life has been transformed over the past twenty years or so.' He knows full well that that's because he had a special talent that was recognised at a key stage. And he's also well aware that there are plenty of former miners still 'sitting around watching day-time television', as he puts it. 'One of them came up to me when we were putting up The Cage and said: "Do you know what? I'd go back down t'pit tomorrow."'

The Cage is one of an increasing number of Malkin sculptures on an impressive scale. 'I did most of it in my garage,' he confides. 'The most difficult part was humping around those blocks of clay.' Mounted on a plinth, it stands some 14 feet high *in situ* – a great clay cube engraved with more mufflered pre-war miners crammed into a winding cage on one side, strikers marching with banners on another, roof supports being erected on the third and a roadway drilling machine of the kind that Harry once serviced on the other. It also stands on another 'village green'. This one's at Allerton Bywater, where the local colliery closed in 1992. Near the former pithead stocks and on the edge of the green is a selection of new Barratt Homes, some of which wouldn't look out of place in Amsterdam. We're only just over eight miles from Leeds and it's not too difficult to see the appeal for would-be commuters of houses starting at under a hundred grand for two bedrooms.

Across the main road is another sign of the times. Where a working men's club used to stand is now the Samuel Valentine Urban Food Hall, offering a selection of fine wines, the products of Yorkshire micro-breweries, a range of local cheeses and cooked meats. Among other things. The menu includes goats' cheese, Mediterranean vegetables and bruschetta, if you please.

Harry orders the home-made pork pie and mushy peas. He may be a successful artist these days, but he's never abandoned his roots. Left Bank? Make that the River Aire, not the Seine. Mind you, he has been mingling with Ed Balls and Yvette Cooper, shadow chancellor and home secretary respectively at time of writing, and the first MPs round here not to have worked in mining. They commissioned him to do a 'small figurative piece' for their garden.

While we're eating, we're briefly joined by Steve Lane, former Fryston face-worker who became rather better known as a rugby league stand-off. He scored well over a hundred tries in a career spanning seventeen years. He played for Dewsbury, Hunslet, Whitehaven and a couple of French teams. Today he's a petroleum broker. Unlike many former sportsmen, he hasn't put on too much weight in middle age. There is about him the gloss of comparative prosperity and the air of restless energy that you tend to find with former miners who weren't ground down by the job. Clutching an open bottle of Australian red, he is waiting to meet someone but seems delighted to bump into Harry and reminisce.

'I used to get up at five for the early shift, leave between one and two and drive all the way to Whitehaven for a seven-thirty kick-off. I'd get in at three a.m., get two hours' kip and then walk a mile to the coalface.'

You know what's coming next. 'They don't know they're born these days,' he confirms. He also remembers scoring four tries at Widnes one Sunday, being concussed and still making it to work in the morning. Then there was the time he broke two fingers playing for Hunslet against Hull Kingston Rovers. 'But I still persuaded the coach to let me play against Bramley on the Wednesday in the Yorkshire Cup. It was 1976 and there was a hundred-quid bonus on offer if we won. We were well ahead when the coach brought me off and somebody in the crowd shouted, "You want your head seeing to playing with your hand strapped up." I told him I'd have played with a broken leg for a hundred quid.'

So what did Steve think working in the pits had given him.

'Character,' he says without hesitation. Then he softens a bit as the aroma of that Aussie wine permeates the atmosphere. 'Fryston was full of characters. And comedians.' Harry nods happily. I don't need to ask what working at the pit gave him. But would he have become the respected artist that he is today without the chance to develop his technique on the rich canvas of his father's broad back?

Opposite page: Harry Malkin's stone mural, modelled on one of Jack Hulme's photographs.

Below: Fryston Colliery bites the dust, as so many more did in the 1980s.

GRIMETHORPE

GRIMETHORPE HAS BEEN the Manchester United of colliery bands in some respects. Not only has it won innumerable honours; its fame has spread far beyond these shores and attracted interest from the great and the good, including movie-makers and composers such as Sir Harrison Birtwistle, who wrote the 'Grimethorpe Aria'. You could also argue that, like Premier League clubs in general and United in particular, it has largely lost touch with its roots – albeit for very different reasons.

It certainly wasn't because Grimethorpe became a wealthy, multinational brand in a global business. Until the phone company Plusnet stepped in with a sponsorship deal in January 2013, the band was in serious danger of folding through lack of funds four years before its centenary. No, Grimethorpe is not the colliery band it was because there are no longer any colliers playing for it. That's hardly surprising. Grimethorpe Colliery was closed twenty years ago, like many another in South Yorkshire.

The announcement was made in the House of Commons on 13 October 1992 by the President of the Board of Trade, Michael Heseltine. Grimethorpe was one name on a very long list. 'I understand the anguish that will be caused in those communities,' intoned Heseltine. 'But there is no economic alternative.' Now where had we heard that phrase before – the one about there being 'no alternative'? Ah, yes, from the previous Prime Minister whose downfall the President had helped to bring about.

At least he was right about one thing in his statement to the Commons. There was more than enough anguish in Grimethorpe that evening. Not least in a band room full of men about to lose their livelihoods. Outside was a media scrum, which completely disrupted rehearsals for the forthcoming national championships. It meant that Grimethorpe's finest arrived at the Royal Albert Hall a few days later somewhat underprepared.

But like a great football manager (a Ferguson or a Busby, perhaps) conductor Frank Renton seized the moment and came up with the right words for what might be termed the pre-match pep talk. 'Win this contest not just for you and Grimethorpe Colliery Band,' he bellowed. 'Win this contest not just for the fifteen hundred miners at Grimethorpe and the village devastated by this announcement. But win this contest for the thirty-three thousand miners nationwide who have just lost their jobs and may, just may, find a little comfort in the knowledge that their band has triumphed in the adversity that afflicts them all, and could just be a glimmer of hope for a very bleak-looking future, whatever they do from then on.'

Renton's team duly went out and won. Cue emotional scenes. Not a dry eye in the house, just like the movies. In fact, those scenes formed the basis for the climax of *Brassed Off*, which came out in 1996 having been largely filmed in Grimethorpe. However entertaining they may be, however, feature films are not real life. They come to an end while life goes on.

Elsie Smith would normally have been at the Albert Hall that day. After all, her husband Bryan had been a star horn soloist in the band and the beneficiary of a football-style transfer in 1964. Having been talent-spotted while moonlighting in a dance band to earn a few extra quid, he had come down from Blackhall Colliery in County Durham with his dad, a euphonium player. They both had the promise of a job at the pit and a Coal Board house in Grimethorpe. But by 1992 Bryan was not well enough to be in London for the triumph of his former bandmates and workmates.

'We had mixed feelings when we heard the news from the Albert Hall,' Elsie recalls. 'Of course we were delighted that Grimethorpe had won, but it didn't take away the worry.' The worry, that is, of what was going to happen next. Like almost every man in the village, Bryan had relied on the pit to earn a living as a joiner on the surface. And like almost every miner in South Yorkshire, the Scargillite heartlands, he had been out on strike for a year from March 1984, in what had turned out to be a failed, last-ditch attempt to stave off colliery closures.

Elsie smiles wanly at a sudden memory of those turbulent years. 'One day Bryan went off to the British Open in Manchester with a fiver in his pocket and strict instructions not to spend it all. We only had about seven pounds to get the whole family through the week during the strike. Well, he came back with the fiver untouched. Mind you, he was taking three steps forward and five back. Turns out that they'd won and everyone wanted to buy them a pint.'

Bryan has since died. 'Biggest funeral Grimethorpe's ever seen. You could hardly get in the church,' says Danny Gillespie, former face-worker and fitter at the pit, in whose front room we're sitting. Danny and Elsie are both pillars of this community. She is chair of the local tenants' and residents' association and secretary of the

Right: Open day at Grimethorpe Colliery, 1993.

Above left: Grimethorpe Colliery band.
Above right: The band after victory at the Albert Hall, 1990s.

Neighbourhood Watch that Danny set up at a time when Grimethorpe was being re-christened 'Crimethorpe' by elements of the national press.

The original name was gift enough to those keen to keep alive the stereotype that the landscape of northern England was all belching chimneys and slagheaps. Soon after the pit closed, Grimethorpe was officially classified as 'the poorest village in England'. Crime shot up from well below the national average to 30 per cent above it. Journalists from serious national newspapers came to report on what was seen as an all-too-typical example of what happens when you take away from a pit village the very reason for its existence.

I was one of them – except that I arrived a few years later when a new century had dawned and things were beginning to change for the better. Elsie had told me

that she knew something had to be done when she saw a youth breaking into an elderly lady's bungalow in the middle of the afternoon. There were similar goings-on at Bolton upon Dearne, another former colliery village in the Borough of Barnsley, where I'd spent a night on patrol with two big-hearted local men trying to protect old people's bungalows in what Sky News had dubbed 'the most burgled road in the country'. Who were they protecting them from? Youths and young men fuelled by drugs and cheap cider – the first generation locally not to follow their fathers into the pits.

Back in Grimethorpe, Danny had decided that enough was enough. He too is a big-hearted man. In fact, he's a big man in every way: well over 6 feet tall and well built. You'd never know that he'd had two heart attacks and suffered from a bad back and knackered knees after working over thirty-five years in the pit, mainly on low seams underground. As he puts it, 'I've spent more of my life crawling than I ever did walking.'

He has never been one to crawl away, however, when confronted by what he would call 'the wrong 'uns'. He knew that he would become a target and be labelled 'a grass' when he went around knocking on doors to raise support for what would later be given first prize in the urban section of the Norwich Union Neighbourhood Watch Awards. After all, the police were hardly popular in these parts after the confrontations during the strike.

'It was the Metropolitan Police who gave us the hassle, not the local bobbies,' Danny insists. 'Our local copper used to live next door to me and his dad was a miner. During the strike, when we didn't have the money to heat our houses, he used to turn a blind eye to us stealing from the stack [coal tip]. In fact, he'd tip us off if his colleagues were planning a raid. "Don't go up there today," he'd say.'

Last time I was here, in December 2000, Danny had pointed out of his front window at the house across the road that had been used during the filming of *Brassed Off*. 'That place on the corner used to be full of druggies,' he'd told me. 'One of them spread nails all over my drive one Friday when I was out at a disco I run for the kiddies. I knew there was something wrong as soon as I pulled in.'

The morning light revealed thirty-eight shining heads embedded in his tyres. When he returned from the garage, there were ten much younger men eyeballing him from the wall across the street. He stood and faced them down and eventually they slunk away. Not so much *Brassed Off* as *High Noon*.

Over twelve years on and Grimethorpe has been transformed in a way that other former South Yorkshire pit villages have not. Thurnscoe, for instance, close to what was Hickleton Main, is 'dying on its feet' according to a local resident interviewed on the Radio Four programme 'A Tale of Two Villages': 'They've built fancy housing but there's no industry.' And that's the key factor.

Danny has picked me up at Barnsley Station this morning and we've driven six miles to the edge of his beloved Grimethorpe. As we get closer, the tarmac looks less worn. These new roads are the vital arteries that pumped blood back into a sclerotic local economy. 'There used to one road in and one road out of this place,' he says, pulling into a lay-by and looking out over the transformed landscape of his former workplace, once a huge mine linked underground to the likes of Darfield Main and Houghton Main.

The 'stack' where he used to go foraging for coal during the strike has been lowered, rounded off and grassed over. And on either side of the road are the functional warehouses and offices of companies producing everything from fitted kitchens and bathrooms to cast-iron fireplaces (for imported coal, presumably).

The biggest employer of all is the most recent arrival, the clothing company ASOS. 'That place where they're based was empty for years,' says Danny. 'We used to call it the white elephant. But they've made a big difference to the employment figures round here.' Male as well as female? 'Oh, yes. A lot of them are employed through agencies, though.' Short contracts, low wages, in other words – exactly the sort of flexible economic conditions that the Thatcher Government had in mind when it decided there was no alternative to taking on the National Union of Mineworkers.

Not too long after the 1997 election, Barnsley Metropolitan Borough Council began working with Yorkshire Forward, a regional development agency backed by the new Labour Government. They began laying down a ribbon of black tarmac that would beckon the twenty-first century into Grimethorpe. What brought in companies like ASOS is the link road connecting the village to the wider world from which it was once so cut off. The road has also brought in buyers for the new detached and semi-detached houses that replaced bulldozed terraces. 'At one time people used to say they wouldn't live in Grimethorpe for a gold pig,' Danny recalls. 'Now they're queueing up to come here. That link road means that they can be in Donny [Doncaster] in twenty minutes and Sheffield in half an hour. You can get to the A1 one way and straight out through Cortonwood to the M1 the other.'

Cortonwood Colliery is now yet another of those retail parks housing everything from Matalan to McDonald's. But it will always be remembered as the site where the bitter dispute of 1984–5 kicked off. Like just about every other former miner in this coalfield, Danny remained loyal to the NUM throughout the year that followed. But that doesn't mean that he's uncritical of Arthur Scargill's tactics or of the behaviour of his more thuggish supporters.

'The worst incident in Grimethorpe was the trashing of the police station house. Then they overturned a police car and set it on fire.' He shakes his head at the memory before going on: 'They were mostly yobs, not real miners. We were involved in a battle to protect our livelihoods. I was fifty at the time with a wife and three kids. I fought for the right to work then and I'd fight for it now, but I still think we went about it the wrong way. There should have been a ballot. As it turned out, she succeeded in dividing us.'

I don't have to tell you to which 'she' Danny is

Iconic image of a miner confronting the Met Police in 1984.

referring. We're now nearly thirty years on from the start of the strike and twenty years from the closure of Grimethorpe Colliery. Does he miss it?

'I did at first. I was in shock for a long time. Mining was a way of life. You could feel things round you that nobody else could feel. It was like a sixth sense. If a bit of stone fell you knew to get out of the way because there'd be a lot more coming. What's more, you made sure that the other blokes got out of the way. You looked after each other down there. Then I think back and I remember that we had no toilets and no washing facilities. You had to carry everything with you, including your water and food. And the air was polluted. You got up in the morning and the windowsill was lined with soot.'

Danny is pushing seventy and admits that he wouldn't be half as fit as he is now had he worked until retirement at sixty-five. As it turned out, the condition of his back, knees and heart meant that he qualified for a 'pit pension' that helped his family to survive financially and gave him the freedom to become an effective campaigner for his community. Apart from

Neighbourhood Watch and involvement with local clubs and associations, he has also been effective as a lobbyist and independent councillor.

Barnsley Council leader Steve Houghton has admitted that other former colliery communities in the borough have not fared so well. 'We can't do everything everywhere to the same extent . . . Grimethorpe was fortunate insofar as it came further down the track [from other redevelopment initiatives] and we learned from our mistakes,' he says before going on to add: 'No one has given up on Thurnscoe, least of all the council.'

Having lost their cinema, swimming baths and market as well as a number of shops, the residents will be glad to hear it. As things stand, it would seem, many of them are distinctly brassed off.

SALLET HOLE AND WATERSAW

THE CLOUDS LOOK LOW ENOUGH TO TOUCH. But then we are high up here on Longstone Edge in the Derbyshire Peak District. And the way Richard Ellis's four-by-four is bouncing around on this rutted track, cratered with muddy puddles the size of small ponds, I feel as though I could be banging my head on those clouds at any minute were it not for the seat belt and the roof over our heads.

To our right is High Rake, Deep Rake and Red Rake, all part of an extensive cliff face running west to east. The crows flapping across it, like gulls over Dover, are picked out in stark relief against light limestone. It's difficult to believe that, as one of those crows flies, Sheffield is only nine miles to the north. To the east is Chesterfield and Buxton lies almost due west.

'DANGER, CLIFF EDGE, STAY AWAY', warns a sign illustrated by the dark outline of a figure plunging to his doom through crumbling rock. Right at the bottom of the valley we can see an immobile yellow digger slightly obscured by a clump of foliage. 'He's on his lunch break,' says Richard.

Around here are the last fluorspar mines in Britain. The cliff face at Longstone Edge is open cast – 'low grade and low cost', according to Richard, who ought to know. He started as a 'diamond driller' working on exploration over forty years ago, did an Open University degree and became a geologist. And, since you ask, being a diamond driller didn't mean that he was drilling for diamonds in Derbyshire; simply that the bit of his drill was impregnated with diamonds. Since 1971 he has been part of a workforce intent on detaching cubes of ore, like sparkling milk teeth, from limestone veins. From those cubes they, in turn, extract fluorspar and grind it into a fine white powder of hydrofluoric acid.

It used to be sold on to chemical companies for use in, among other things, non-stick pans, welding rods, asthma inhalers, glass etching and mobile phones. But Glebe Mines, the company that Richard still works for two days a week, was recently bought by a Sardinian company called Fluorsid that needs fluorspar to process aluminium. So Glebe have changed their name to British Fluorspar and resumed underground mining at Milldam under nearby Hucklow Edge after a break of over thirteen years. 'It's been on care and maintenance since 1999,' says Richard – or Fred, as the miners prefer to call him. 'I think they thought Richard was a bit posh,' he confides. Well, at least they didn't call him Dick or Ed or, worse still, run both names together.

I ask Richard (or Fred) why Milldam was mothballed in the first place.

'There were easier pickings elsewhere,' Richard suggests. One was the open-cast option that is still going on despite sustained opposition from the Save Longstone Edge campaign. Environmental issues are always going to be pressing in an area such as

The extensive cliff face at
Longstone Edge.

this. Before permission was granted to resume mining at Milldam, a report had to be prepared for the Peak National Authority. It cost £150,000 to commission and turned out to be twice as thick as the average encyclopedia. Even then the motion to allow the resumption was passed by just one vote.

The other option was drift mining – walking into a tunnel or 'adit' rather than hurtling 800 feet or so down a shaft to work in the bowels of the earth.

We're on our way to see Watersaw, a drift mine that closed as recently as 2008, as we bounce across the top of High Rake. On the horizon beyond the far side of the cliff face, Richard points out the winding-house chimney from one of many former lead mines that abounded in these parts until the 1950s. 'After two thousand years they were pretty well worked out,' he says. And just to the left is a police mast that replaced the pithead to Ladywash, another underground fluorspar

reopened,' says Richard.

It was put on 'care and maintenance' not too long after a freak flood at one of the nearby 'lagoons' – ponds the size of small reservoirs where the waste or 'tailings' are pumped into and stored before being dredged out and used for backfilling those great holes in the landscape caused by mining. One of the lagoons had not been dredged for thirty-five years and an excess of rainwater caused it to overflow and spill into a nearby fish pond.

So it came to pass that Brian Greenan, the weighbridge operator at Glebe's headquarters in Cavendish Mill, looked out of his window one day to see water cascading towards him and sweeping all before it. 'I noticed some rather fine crucian carp in there and, being an angler and a fish keeper, I knew how to revive them,' he told me. 'I managed to empty a dustbin, fill it with water and keep alive three out of the four that I rescued.

Right: A misty dawn on Longstone Edge.

mine that closed in 1979. Around 120 miners worked there at the time, most of them from local villages.

There were far fewer at Watersaw nearly twenty years on. When the four-by-four finally comes to a halt and I clamber out to stretch my much-jolted backbone, it feels as though we've just arrived in a Wild West settlement evacuated on news that a notorious gang of gunslingers are heading for town. Debris from an abandoned workplace is strewn about. Shacks of corrugated iron – offices, fitting shops or whatever – are rusting away. In some cases, bits of wall or roof have fallen off. There's rust too on the locked metal gates to the mine itself.

So why hasn't this area been cleared up a bit over the past five years or so?

'Well, there's still a chance that it might be

I've still got them in my pond at home. They were lucky fish.'

Residents of nearby Stoney Middleton were not so lucky, however. Down the hill flowed the murky torrent, coating the village in a deposit of up to 3 feet of sludge. The clean-up operation cost around £2 million. Glebe Mines were fined £22,000 and ordered to pay another £16,937 to the Environment Agency. They went out of business in 2010 at a cost of sixty-six jobs. Only temporarily, as it happens. Thanks to the Sardinians, they're now back in business under a new name.

Mine manager Rob Ridley was gearing up for the restart of mining at Milldam when I called in at Cavendish Mill in October 2012. But he still found time to reminisce about his early years as a miner at Watersaw and Sallet Hole, another drift mine further down the valley. 'We all moved up to Watersaw some time in the eighties when Sallet Hole was worked out,' he told me. And by 'all' he means 120 miners, including a fair number of his family – his father, a couple of uncles and a cousin or three. The Ridleys came on the bus from Chesterfield with former coal miners who had switched to fluorspar when their pits closed. 'A lot of them said it was tougher mining hard rock in wet conditions,' Rob recalled.

It's a contentious view and one that some coal miners would discount with derision. They often had to crawl around low seams in dusty conditions with the ever-present threat of leaking gas and falling rock. Let's just acknowledge that they were both tough jobs and leave it at that.

Young Ridley was twenty-one when he started at Sallet Hole in 1977. 'I'd already trained as a bricklayer because my dad wanted me to have another trade,' he explained. There was good money in bricklaying, then

calcite and a dark line of lead sulphide, or galena, one of the by-products sold on to a Belgian company for smelting.

Getting at fluorspar sounds like a similar process to tin mining in Cornwall – a lot of blasting and drilling with much noise and vibration. 'White finger was quite common,' Rob remembered. It was also known to medics as hand-arm vibration syndrome (HAVS) and to other miners as 'dead finger', the blood vessels, nerves, muscles and joints being affected. As the condition suggests, the drills were hand-held, which was even more difficult if you happened to be up a ladder at the time. 'Once you'd walked into a drift mine, you could be going up or down,' he explained. 'There were five different sub-levels and some of the seams were quite a few feet above your head.'

About as close as the clouds seemed on High Ridge. Mind you, the clouds had cleared by the time I

Left: An industrial process in the beautiful setting of the Derbyshire peaks.

and now, and fluorspar mining wasn't badly paid either. He was soon earning over seventy quid a week, a decent wage in those days.

It's not difficult to imagine what he looked like at the time, perhaps because he has the slightly greying hairstyle of Rod Stewart in his pomp. There's something of the 1970s, too, about Rob's office. Maybe it's the abundance of thick grey files on high shelves, or maybe it's the map of Europe with the Union of Soviet Socialist Republics dominating the eastern half. It's the office of a man, one suspects, who would rather be out at the rock face than sitting in front of a computer screen.

Talking of rock, he seems to have quite a few lumps either on his desk or tucked away nearby. He lets me take home a chunk of ore in which those tooth-like cubes of fluorspar are evident below a spiky exterior of

finally bade farewell and set off down the steep narrow lane towards Stoney Middleton. The sun was filtering through the trees and the timeless beauty of the Peak District reasserted itself. Cavendish Mill might have belonged to a different planet beyond the clouds as it geared up to process the first tub-loads of the getting on for two million tons of crude ore that Richard reckons are there to be truffled out of Milldam. High-grade crude ore, he might add, unlike the open-cast variety at Longstone Edge.

Sardinians willing, it looks as though fluorspar mining will be going on round here for some time yet, whether the environmentalists or the local residents like it or not.

COTGRAVE

A SPADE IS AN UNUSUAL IMPLEMENT to find slotted into a window frame in a parish church. Now I was a teenage gravedigger in the summer of 1969 and, believe me, this spade is too dainty to have dug anything deep enough to accommodate a coffin. It's small and polished and gleaming in the light funnelling through stained glass at All Saints in the Nottinghamshire village of Cotgrave. The window is dedicated to 'those who gave their skill, energy, health and sometimes life itself to the mining of coal beneath the land of this parish'. And beneath the spade is a plaque pointing out that it was 'presented to Her Royal Highness Princess Margaret on the occasion of the cutting of the first sod of the new colliery at Cotgrave on April 7th, 1954'.

Surprisingly enough, she didn't take it home to do a little light weeding in the gardens of Kensington Palace. And between you and me, she didn't really insert the spade in the spot where the shaft was to be sunk. Officials had to move her to an adjacent field, which was rather less muddy. Still, at least the local press got their pictures.

I'm looking at one now. There's the Queen's late sister in long fur coat and matching hat with one very high-heeled shoe resting on the blade of the spade. A wheelbarrow is positioned nearby, presumably just in case she decided to set to with the vigour of a colliery shaft sinker. Unlikely.

I'm also looking at a photograph taken almost exactly forty years later. It's dated 1994, but no month is specified. At first sight it could be showing the demolition of two tower blocks. Look a bit closer, however, and it's evident that those towers are too small to have accommodated many council flats. They are, or rather were, the structures encasing the Koepe hoisting gear, a modern, almost science-fiction alternative to the traditional colliery winding gear. Very 1960s. Unlikely as it seems, that game-changing decade was well under way by the time Cotgrave was open for business, a full nine years after HRH's staged sod-turning.

Princess Margaret posing for the cameras as work on Cotgrave Colliery begins.

There were problems from the start, not least the sheer quantity of water underground. Around the bottom of the shaft was enough to form an underground lake. A specialist refrigeration company had to be brought in to freeze it long enough for the surrounding tunnels to be adequately lined.

The 60s, however, was an optimistic period and managers remained confident that they had struck black gold. Nottinghamshire has always had plentiful supplies of coal. After all, it was the ground above which Sherwood Forest was once widely spread. At its peak, this coalfield produced 25 million tons of coal a year and half its pits qualified for the million-tons-a-year league. But the vast majority were in the north of the county. Cotgrave is six miles south of the city of Nottingham, in the comparatively prosperous borough of Rushcliffe and not too far from the vast coal deposits under the picturesque Vale of Belvoir.

'Like the Third Reich, the pit was supposed to last for a thousand years,' says

author and collier's son Duncan Hamilton. As it turned out, it was worked for exactly thirty. It closed for good in 1993, by which time the workforce was down to about 500 – less than a third of what it had been at its peak. Duncan's relationship with his father, a miner and a Newcastle United fan, is the catalyst for his most recent book *The Footballer Who Could Fly*. Hamilton senior was one of many miners from the Northeast who came to Cotgrave for what they assumed would be a more secure future. Others came from Wales, Scotland, Yorkshire, Derbyshire and elsewhere. Such was the diversity of accents and dialects that special classes had to be held so that miners from soon-to-be-closed Nottingham collieries, such as Radford and Clifton, could understand the incomers and there were no potentially dangerous misunderstandings underground.

Unlike the majority of the incomers, the Hamiltons were rather too early to avail themselves of one of the thousand or so new Coal Board houses built on a sizeable estate that was grafted on to the then ancient heart of Cotgrave in the 1960s. Instead they lived at nearby Keyworth, a village bisected by the Nottingham Road. 'Our side was the council estate and every second house was occupied by someone who worked at the pit,' Duncan recalls. 'The bus taking the miners to work used to leave from outside the barber's shop at the top of the road.'

The younger Hamilton would eventually travel a little further to work at the word-face, cutting his teeth as a journalist on what was then the *Nottingham Evening Post*. As the football correspondent covering Nottingham Forest, his sometimes turbulent relationship with Brian Clough was the basis for *Provided You Don't Kiss Me*, one of two of his works to win the William Hill Sports Book of the Year award.

The other was his consummate biography of Harold Larwood. Destined to be the main weapon in England's so-called 'bodyline' tour of Australia in 1932–3, Larwood was a terrifying fast bowler and one of a veritable production line of Nottinghamshire cricketers who came out of the pits. Annesley Colliery alone forged five future England players, including Larwood's partner in terror, Bill Voce, a man so strong that he could allegedly rip a tobacco tin in half with his bare hands.

Annesley was close to Kirkby-in-Ashfield in the north of the county. I remember it well, as I remember Clipstone, Tibshelf, Newstead and many another mining community because I, too, worked for the *Post* – in the 1970s, as it happens, before Duncan's arrival. Fond memories come flooding back. Of writing colour pieces

about mining galas; of listening to pigeon fanciers explain how their pride and joy would find its way from a Scottish hillside to a back yard just outside Mansfield; of being allowed to wind a wheel pulling a wire attached to a piece of fur pursued by frenzied whippets; of sitting in on colliery band rehearsals and listening to a respected elder of this most competitive form of music remark: 'He's gorra lovely lip, that horn player.'

By the mid-80s, I had long left the area. I could only look on, appalled and saddened, as television cameras showed the mining communities that I'd known being torn apart. Mass pickets and armies of state-sponsored police clashed at the gates of those pits, and we all know why. The majority of Nottinghamshire miners had refused to join the national strike on the grounds that there had never been a ballot. They broke away from the National Union of Mineworkers to form the Union of Democratic Mineworkers. And much good it did them! Collieries here were closed down along with collieries elsewhere because the destruction of the British coal industry was part of the political agenda.

We shall return to the UDM because there's no escaping from it in any discussion of mining in Notts. First let me introduce Mike Astill, an old friend, former colleague on the *Post* and the *Nottingham News*, author

of *Nottinghamshire, A Portrait in Colour*, and long-term Cotgrave resident. His wife Sheila is a churchwarden and their son Stephen plays for the local colliery welfare football club, having married a former miner's daughter.

Like most of today's residents on the expansive estate of properties once rented out by the Coal Board, the junior Astills are buying their house. 'At least there's a shop here now, and a hairdresser's.' Mike points out two converted former houses as we circumnavigate what you might call the outer ring road in his car. 'For a long time after the estate was built, there were no facilities.' Apart that is from 'the club', as the colliery welfare has always been known. We're due there at 2 p.m. after a bacon sandwich and a tramp across the snow covering the country park that now surrounds the site of the former mine.

'It's beautiful here in the summer,' Mike assures me. 'People who used to look down on Cotgrave as a mining village now visit in some numbers.' The colliery site itself is fenced off from the rest of the park and, despite today's white coating, it's evidently nowhere near as attractive. Barratt Homes have planning permission to build 440 new houses there. 'Private property – Keep out', says a sign on a fence beyond which are some snow-covered dustbin bags. 'This is a closed colliery site.

Persons entering will be trespassing and may be exposing themselves to danger.'

Not half so much danger, one suspects, as the men faced on a daily basis when this was an open colliery site. There were ten deaths here between 1959, while exploratory work was still going on, and 1989. Causes ranged from being caught in machinery to being crushed by a coal-cutter. Electrocution also featured.

Stephen Astill's father-in-law, Alan Parry, who is waiting to meet us at the club, would be the first to admit that his back injury, in October 1985, was comparatively minor. But the damage to three discs in his spine was enough to have him moved from the coalface to working on the surface. When the closure came eight years later, he kept turning up for work every day and clocking in. He had been one of 56 Cotgrave men to join the strike (out of 1,500) and maintains: 'I was refusing to leave the job I'd fought for. Calverton [to the east of Nottingham] was still open and Asfordby [just outside Melton Mowbray] had just opened. I wanted a job at one of them, but they didn't want a man with a bad back. Eventually the management took me to Mansfield for a medical and I was declared unfit for life. At least it meant that I got a

decent pension and invalidity benefit.'

He hasn't worked since. Not at a colliery, nor anywhere else. 'I applied for plenty of jobs but, when they found out about the back injury, nobody wanted to know,' he says. Bear in mind he was forty at the time Cotgrave closed and he's only fifty-nine now.

Alan was just eighteen months old in 1954 when his father came down from Doncaster to help dig the shaft that Princess Margaret had almost begun. He has the speech patterns of a man of Nottinghamshire yet considers himself to be a Yorkshireman. 'It's no different from people whose dads come from Wales or Scotland claiming that they're Welsh or Scottish,' he insists.

The club bar is sparsely populated this afternoon. 'When the pit was open, this room would have been packed with men coming off the day shift, while others would be having a couple of pints before going home for a kip before the night shift,' says Ron Murphy, who came down here from Dawdon Colliery at Seaham, near Sunderland, in 1969.

There are two other former Durham coalfield men in the bar as well. Also nursing pints are Michael Gladwin, whose mining roots are buried over the border

in Derbyshire, and Mick Chewings, who was fifteen in 1966 when his father moved here from South Wales.

A fairly typical gathering of Nottinghamshire mining employees then, you might imagine. Yet there's not one former member of the UDM present. Of the six men supping, two were deputies, one a surveying assistant, while three were face-workers and proud members of the NUM.

Michael's two brothers continued to work through the strike. 'Blood's thicker than water and we get on OK,' he reflects. 'But they couldn't look at me when I was on the picket line and they were crossing it.' He takes a swig of his beer before going on: 'To this day, if I go to Blackpool and there's a bar full of Yorkshiremen, I'd never tell them that I was a Notts miner. How could I prove that I was out on strike?'

At this point Mick, a proud Welshman, comes up with a startling statistic: 'I can't speak for the rest of the county, but at this pit the vast majority of the fifty-six who supported the strike were Nottinghamshire born and bred. It was mainly the older ones who stayed in – the ones who'd come from other parts of Britain for what they thought was the security of a job for life.'

Left: Cotgrave Colliery in the optimistic 1960s.

Above: Digging for coal, 1990s.

Alan and Michael are in staunch agreement on that point. Which rather complicates the assumptions that continue to underlie the chants on the football terraces of Sheffield and Chesterfield to this day (mainly parroted by youths and young men who weren't even born at the time) that Notts miners were all 'scabs'.

Needing to earn money for the first time in a year, Mick and Michael set to work with a will after the strike. Alan, too, until his accident. 'The atmosphere among the blokes was never quite the same afterwards,' says Michael sadly. But, despite Cotgrave's increasingly evident geological faults, they shifted some coal. 'On one seam we were working an hour and twenty minutes from the pit bottom,' Mick recalls. 'We could have been breaking into the new workings at Asfordby if they hadn't closed us down.'

Asfordby, across the Leicestershire border, was Britain's newest colliery. It was also the most short-lived, having opened in 1993 and closed four years later, and those huge coal deposits under the Vale of Belvoir remained largely undisturbed. Attempts to get at them from this shaft just outside Melton were thwarted by more geological faults. Back in the late 1970s and early 80s, an alliance of farmers, hunters, Stilton cheese-makers and the Duke of Rutland had successfully persuaded government ministers that no shaft could be sunk in the heart of such a picturesque and wealthy landscape.

Cotgrave Colliery Welfare is just over fifteen miles from the Duke's Belvoir Castle, but it feels like part of another planet. As we know, the club's still open (just about) and the football team is still going. But the cricket team, like many another, is suffering from the sidelining of the game in state schools. No longer can it rely on fast bowlers and big-hitters coming out of the pits – big-hitters such as Gerry Hopper, who has just walked into the club bar.

Back in the 60s he won an *Evening Post* competition for the club cricketer to hit the most sixes in a season. Twenty-one, since you ask. 'That included twelve in one game,' he shrugs. 'We were playing Hucknall at the time.'

Hucknall was another colliery town. We can only assume that their team at the time lacked the bowling firepower of Annesley in the 1920s when Larwood and Voce were on their way from the coalface to Nottinghamshire's Trent Bridge ground and eventually into cricketing immortality.

Miners taking the underground
to work.

DESFORD

TAFFY'S TEETH DIDN'T STAND A CHANCE. One minute they were there, resting on his 'snap' tin while he tucked into a sandwich (for some reason he took them out to eat). The next minute they were gone. Blown away, you might say, by what amounted to an underground hurricane.

The cause was not unexpected. Miners at Desford Colliery in Leicestershire had been waiting for a substantial fall of rock in the wake of the relentless advance of their newfangled hydraulic roof support. That was to be expected. It was part of mining. What they hadn't foreseen was the sheer volume of noise and force of wind created by 150 yards of roof coming down all at once. It had never happened before. Not when roofs were held up by simple wooden props that had to be assembled by hand, making progress considerably slower.

'We were working on the other face, at least two miles away, but I'll never forget that noise,' says former Desford miner Barrie Sutton.

'Nor me,' puts in his old pal Mick Goddard, a colliery electrician. 'It made your hair stand on end and I was a fair way from it as well. Men closer to it were thrown over on their faces when it cropped [collapsed].'

Thankfully, nobody was seriously injured, but Taffy's top and bottom set were never found again. He had to go back to driving his tunnelling machine temporarily toothless. From a distance of some fifty years, neither Barrie nor Mick can remember his second name but, judging by his nickname, we can hazard a guess at his origins. Welsh, Scots, Lancastrians and others migrated to the Midlands in some numbers in the post-war years as pits in their own areas were worked out. 'We had a lot of Irish as well,' Barrie recalls. 'They used to come on the bus from Leicester [nine miles to the east]. Five double-deckers there were every day. And the bike shed in the fifties seemed to go on forever.' Evidently you had to take careful note of where you'd parked your bicycle or you might never find it again.

The Leicestershire coalfield was booming at the time. That was particularly true of Desford, which had well over 2,000 employees. As the 1950s gave way to the 60s, it would find itself in the forefront of technological advance. 'Even before all that came in, we'd regularly turned a million tons a year with nothing more than picks and shovels,' Barrie points out. By 'we' he means Desford number one and number two shafts and the nearby Merrylees drift mine, two tunnels driven in the early 1940s to boost wartime production. 'We were like separate mines when I first went there as a pit-pony lad in 1955,' he goes on. 'Number one and number two men would sit in separate parts of the canteen. We'd also play each other at football. But by the end of the fifties we were all connected up.'

The invention of that first hydraulic roof support came a few years later. It became known as the 'Desford Chock' and its use would spread far beyond the borders of Leicestershire. 'Our under-manager, a bloke called Matt Smith, came up with the idea,' Mick suggests.

Barrie nods. 'It was that shape,' he explains, pointing to an archway across Mick's front room. 'It just expanded like a bloody big mushroom that slotted under the curve of the roof. Yes, it was Matt's idea, but I'm not sure if he patented it. Certainly it was Dowty's [the mining equipment company] that took it on and developed it.'

Did it make your life easier?

'Oh, yes. It meant that you didn't need to keep propping up the roof. Mind you, the Coal Board discouraged us from going the full hundred and fifty yards again.'

The introduction of the Anderton Shearer Loader was another labour-saver. Patented in 1953 by James Anderton OBE, who later became chairman of the NCB's North-Western Division, it would prove to be a double-edged coal-cutting machine for Barrie. 'It could do in ten

minutes what used to take me hours,' he says. 'Instead of using a pick and shovel after putting in gelignite and shot-firing, you just sheared it off the face. When I first started, there were twenty-two men responsible for eight yards each. The seams were four-foot-six high and each man was expected to come out with roughly twenty tons over an eight-hour shift. You had to crawl to get to your "ratch" [section of the face].'

Not easy on the knees, of course. By a cruel irony, however, it was an accident with one of those labour-saving power loaders that did the most damage. 'I was dragged under it and it nearly had my leg off,' he reflects. 'I was off the face for some time. The other day I went to see the doctor in Leicester about my knees. He saw the scar and asked me how much I'd got in compensation. "Around five hundred quid," I said, and he shook his head. He reckoned I'd get the best part of forty grand in a

similar workplace accident today.'

Well, maybe, but it couldn't happen at any colliery in Leicestershire. Apart from some recent open-cast activity around Measham, mining here has been and gone. Desford closed in February 1984, shortly before the beginning of the national strike. Geological faults were blamed. At the time, the colliery was as old as the century itself, having been sunk in 1900. Some of the Desford miners went to work at Asfordby, Britain's newest and shortest-lived colliery, sited near Melton Mowbray some forty minutes drive away. Barrie, who had recently qualified as a deputy, moved to Donisthorpe on the border with South Derbyshire. And having worked at several Leicestershire mines, Mick spent the last eleven years of his working life at a quarry.

'It was never the same, though,' he reflects, and Barrie nods knowingly. When you ask them what they miss, the answer is as predictable as ever but no less touching. They miss the comradeship of life underground where men looked out for each other and helped each other out where necessary. 'Some men could shift eight yards of coalface quicker than others,' says Barrie, 'but the slower ones weren't just left to get on with it.'

That generosity of spirit, that selflessness, has been less evident in wider society since the 1980s, when the decision was taken to close down most of Britain's coal industry. Today just happens to be the day after the outgoing head of Ofgem, Alistair Buchanan, has warned that energy prices are set to soar because we're too reliant on imports. Closing the few remaining coal-fired power stations makes sense environmentally, but we haven't done enough to replace them. The options are limited, largely because of rampant Nimbyism. It's perhaps understandable that nobody wants a nuclear

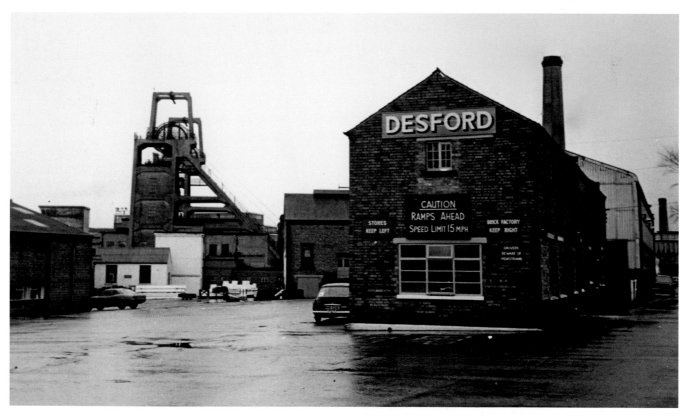

Left: Emerging from Desford pit.   **Above:** Desford Colliery, 1983.

power station in their back yard – and certainly not a nuclear waste dump. But nobody wants any 'fracking' for gas nearby either. As for wind farms, we don't want them despoiling our landscape, thank you very much.

I've just been to see the Desford site in the genial company of Andrew Furlong, head of external relations at the Institute of Chemical Engineers and an enthusiastic student of mining history, who happens to live in the next village. We're well within the boundaries of the National

Forest, where any number of deciduous and coniferous trees have been planted. It's a glorious February day with a hint of spring in the air and it's not difficult to imagine that, in a few years time, the forest will be decked out in some finery.

As it is, it's difficult to believe that there was ever a working pit on this site. The commemorative winding wheel is just about visible on an island surrounded by what has become a rather pleasant fishing lake with a sturdy seat on the side. At the bottom of the lane, the local brickworks is equally well hidden. A horse-rider resplendent in bright yellow jacket has just trotted past en route to the track through the trees. 'Fishing, cycling, horse-riding: welcome to the post-industrial leisure economy,' Andrew muses with perhaps a faint hint of irony.

Like me, he finds it all very scenic and environmentally sound. But also like me, he's worried that increasing numbers of UK citizens are struggling to heat their homes. He has already stood as the Labour candidate for the parliamentary constituency of Bosworth in 1997 and 2001. On both occasions he took the incumbent Tory MP David Tredinnick to a recount – quite an achievement, even at the zenith of Blairism, in an area of such plumply prosperous farmland.

Having met me up at Nuneaton Station, we've driven over the A5 Warwickshire border, headed past Bosworth Field and then through Market Bosworth, a classic slice of Middle England that could quite easily have been transported from the Home Counties. As we continue in a northwesterly direction, however, the towns and villages take on a more work-a-day appearance. There are pockets of former Coal Board housing and Victorian miners' rows here and there. 'The culture here in Leicestershire was not greatly changed by the existence of deep coal mining to the extent that it was in, say, South Yorkshire,' says Andrew. 'Mind you, there's a terraced street down here,' he adds, swinging to the left, 'where they used to hang washing across the street when I first came in the late eighties.'

There wouldn't have been much chance of it staying too clean, I would have thought, in the days when South Leicester Colliery was going full tilt at the bottom of this street. Pretty well all that's left today is another of those commemorative winding wheels, quite an ornate affair with latticework spokes through which we can see a children's playground and a church across wide-open fields.

Despite the name, we're not in South Leicester at all, or any other part of Leicester for that matter. The city is still quite a few miles to the east. We're in the heart of Ellistown but, equally confusing, the former Ellistown pit was out of town. The shafts have been capped and the site covered with trees opposite what is now the headquarters of a company offering 'a palletised delivery network across Europe'. Nailstone Colliery, meanwhile, appears to have been on the edge of Battram. There's absolutely nothing left of it. 'I think the site is marked to be a waste management scheme,' says Andrew. Certainly it could do with some litter management at the moment. The padlocked and barbed-wired gateway to the former site is strewn with cider cans, McDonald's boxes, dumped black bags and even a discarded window frame.

All these pits, including nearby Bagworth, closed in the 1980s or early 90s. Slightly to the north of here is Coalville, the name of which speaks for itself. It was the administrative headquarters of the Leicestershire coalfield and the site of Whitwick (1824 to 1986) and Snibston (1833 to 1983), mines which were connected underground in the 1960s. Snibston was founded by George Stephenson, who was in the area in 1830 with his son Robert, supervising the construction of the Leicester to Swannington Railway. Having cast a judicious eye over the thriving operation at Whitwick, George and his partners sank two shafts in quick succession. He also brought in experienced miners

Above: The commemorative winding wheel is just about visible on an island surrounded by a fishing lake.

from his native Northumberland and set them and their families up in six rows of miners' cottages. Some of his employees were just ten years old, but a schoolroom was provided for younger children and it doubled as a chapel on Sundays. Today's children (and their parents) now have a 'Discovery Park' at their disposal on the site of the former pit, deep in the heart of the National Forest.

Back in Mick's front room in Newbold Verdon, meanwhile, he and Barrie are still enjoying their reminiscences of life at nearby Desford Colliery. 'Remember the time that horse chased you,' Barrie chortles.

'I knew you'd bring that up,' his mate responds with the air of a man who's been trying to bury the memory for half a century.

Barrie, though, is in full flow. 'He came on to

our face to do a bit of maintenance work at snap time. Normally we'd tether up the pony but, on this occasion, we thought we'd have a bit of fun. We let it go and it fell in behind Mick and started following him. It must have spooked him a bit because he broke into a run and so did the horse.'

'I could shift a bit in those days,' Mick insists.

'So could the horse.' Barrie is in fits by this stage.

The victim of this jolly jape is grinning himself by now as he remembers diving into a hole to escape the relentless pounding of hooves. But, just in case you're wondering, he didn't find any false teeth down there.

COVENTRY

COVENTRY COLLIERY, KERESLEY, OR KERESLEY PIT, COVENTRY: take your pick. They were two sides of the same major access point to the rich, thick bed of coal under Warwickshire. Keresley 'village', as the colliery estate has always been known, is within the northwestern boundaries of Coventry. Yet it has always felt like a place apart.

The rest of the city was, for a while, the New Jerusalem of the post-war world. Men came from all over the UK and Ireland – particularly Ireland – to rebuild after the blitz. Their families followed. More men came to help construct the elevated ring road that was seen as essential to carry the growing numbers of cars, most of them being turned out in thriving factories. It was, after all, a boom town, as the Specials gloomily reminded us in 1981. By the time their haunting and most apposite single was at number one in the charts, urban riots were raging and the decimation of manufacturing was in full swing. National journalists were taking day returns from Euston to compose pre-ordered obituaries for the conveniently labelled 'Ghost Town'.

The decimation of coal mining was still to come, in Coventry as elsewhere. Like the rest of the city, Keresley was full of people from somewhere else. 'Warwickers', as those born and bred within the confines of the Warwickshire coalfield were known, were very much a minority – although, as time went on, the accents of the sons and grandsons of the incomers owed more to the West Midlands than to the West of Scotland, West and South Yorkshire, Durham, Lancashire or South Wales. Mining had begun here in 1917 and, not too long afterwards, hardened colliers and their families began arriving from worked-out pits hundreds of miles away.

The Welsh, incidentally, were particularly prevalent at Binley Colliery on the east side of the city. Hence the legacy of the Binley Male Voice Choir, which survived long after the closure of the pit in 1963 and evolved into the City of Coventry Male Voice Choir nearly thirty years later. I remember meeting a bunch of former Binley miners in a pub some time in the 1980s and being richly entertained. Not by their singing so much as their colourful stories, their rich humour and sheer *joie de vivre*, or whatever the Welsh equivalent of that phrase is. The mine had been closed for over twenty years and most of them had been working in factories until they, too, started to close. But it was still the former colliers' shared life underground that marked them out as a special breed of men.

At that time I was features editor and columnist on what was still the *Coventry Evening Telegraph*. We had a demanding editor of the old school and a staff full of ambitious youngsters who were keen to learn. Many would eventually take a one-way ticket to Euston and establish themselves among the brightest and best journalists of their generation. Among those who stayed was a talented cricket and rugby writer called Steve Evans, a local lad from Keresley and the first on the male side of his family to earn a living at the word-face rather than the coalface.

'My dad always pledged that "none of my lads will ever work down the pit"', Steve recalls. And you can understand why when he tells the story of his father and grandfather. Both were called Jim and both survived to the age of eighty-five against all the odds. Jim Evans senior had worked at Spennymoor Colliery in Durham and started work as a shot-firer at Keresley in 1927 after moving his family south with all their worldly possessions piled on a coal cart, appropriately enough. 'He was drilling holes in rock without any protection or face mask,' his grandson says. 'Apparently he was paid a shilling for every hole he drilled. All that dust and nothing protecting his mouth, and all those Woodbines once he was back on the surface. Yet Granddad lived to a ripe old age. Great lungs.'

Jim junior went down the pit as a young teenager. Among miners everyone had a nickname and his was 'Jackpot' in later life because he was lucky on the one-armed bandit and the bingo in the social club. Perhaps he deserved a bit of luck in that regard because he didn't have much elsewhere. Having joined the Territorial Army, he was one of the first called up in 1939. What happened after that? Well, as they used to say on the back page of the old *Cov Tel*, Steve Evans reports:

'He served with the 1st/7th Royal Warwickshire Regiment and they were sacrificial lambs. While the British retreating troops were cowering on the Dunkirk beaches, awaiting salvation from the little ships, the Royal Warwicks were ordered to defend the perimeter to prevent the Germans from completing the slaughter. Dad was one of only seven survivors. He spent the rest of the war as a POW and, in 1945, had to endure the infamous Long March from Poland to Germany in winter. Eventually he was liberated and returned to bomb-ravaged Coventry a slim Jim weighing about seven stone. He found employment in the only job he knew – back down the pit with his dad.'

Jim junior spent another forty years working at Keresley. 'He used to drive the Dosco,' Steve goes on, 'cutting swathes of coal from the face. On one occasion the Dosco went into reverse and trapped him. He escaped with a few broken ribs.'

Those of us who never had to go to war or down the pit should perhaps count our blessings at this point. Then we might ask what it was about Coventry Colliery that made men like Jim Evans senior up sticks and move to the Midlands. The obvious answer is that the pits nearer to their homes were often worked out, or not far off it, while the thick, high seams here seemed to offer coal ad infinitum. But there was more to it than that.

By the standards of some colliery owners, the

Warwickshire Coal Company was considered a good employer. They built decent houses for the miners, more spacious than most, with inside toilets. Whatever next? Baths to keep their coal in? In 1924 the social club was opened, with sporting and cultural activities second to none. Apart from cricket and football pitches, there were tennis courts and an Italianate garden with an ornate bandstand at its heart and rehearsal rooms for the colliery band underneath.

'It was about where that five-a-side pitch is now,' says Russell Woffendin as we peer through the fence from the main road through Keresley on a sharp, clear

Sunday morning. Now in his eighties, Russell started work at the colliery in 1947, finished up as a deputy and retired in 1984. Today he's sporting a rather natty trilby with a flourishing brown feather stitched into the hat band – a Robin Hood hat, no less. He's also wearing trainers, which seem a bit odd for an octogenarian on such a cold morning until he casually drops out in conversation that one foot had been crushed by a 'Panzer' and the only remaining toe is the little one. A Panzer, in this case at least, is a coalface conveyor belt rather than a tank.

Russell was a useful cricketer in his day, able to generate some pace as a bowler. 'I was nowhere near as fast as my dad, though,' he admits. 'Pads weren't much protection if you were hit on the shin by him.' Douglas Woffendin came down from Ossett, West Yorkshire, in 1932 and proceeded to put the fear of God into visiting batsmen, be they playing against Keresley, Griff & Coton in the Coventry Works League or – all too briefly – for Warwickshire in the County Championships.

Like many a former Yorkshire miner, it seems, he was not slow in voicing his opinions. And when county captain Peter Cranmer asked him to bowl on a drying, uncovered, spinner's wicket after a heavy burst of rain, he told him in no uncertain terms that it was a daft idea. Cranmer had been to Christ Church College,

Oxford, played rugby union for England, and would go on to become a major in the war. He did not tolerate insubordination from a mere 'player'.

At least the management at Keresley could see Woffendin's value. Rather than risk injury to their prime cricketing asset, he was moved from the coalface and found a job on the ground staff. Works cricket was a serious business in those days. At least the pitch is still there, looking as forlorn as cricket fields tend to do in midwinter. There's a bowling green, too, and a couple of football pitches. 'They had a match there yesterday afternoon,' Russell assures me. 'The playing fields were left to the village in perpetuity.'

But not the tennis courts, it would seem. They were covered with car park tarmac some years ago. No cars on there today, however, apart from mine. When the pit was working, members would already be gathering outside the club at this time on a Sunday waiting for that magic noontime sound of internal keys being turned and bolts springing back.

Alas, the club has been closed since 2012 and has since been demolished. It was losing £500 a week. Maybe the miracle is that it lasted so long. After all, the colliery itself closed in 1991, putting 1,300 men out of work. Record production levels of over a million tons a year meant nothing. John Major's government was no less intransigent than Margaret Thatcher's when it came to the miners. The decision had been made that Britain's energy needs must be met from other sources, even if that meant importing coal to a country and, in this case, a county with more deposits than most beneath its surface. Coventry Colliery made a brief comeback under private ownership with far fewer employees, but by 1996 it had closed for good. The Homefire smokeless fuel plant lasted another four years, fed by coal from elsewhere. It had dominated the Keresley skyline for forty years.

Well, at least the pit wheel has made a comeback. Half of it at least is visible above ground as a monument to the men who worked here. There's not much else to look at these days, apart from the Prologis Business Park. 'This was the main gate to the pit,' says former face-worker Graham Borrows as we stand staring across at the faceless frontages of those warehouses. 'There used to be anything up to five hundred coppers on the other gate during the strike,' he goes on.

The year-long stoppage of 1984–5 was a terrible time for Keresley village. Mass pickets were mounted to try to stop the few miners who continued to work from the start. As so often, the bitterness lingered long afterwards on an estate where families had known one another for generations. Hostility towards nearby Daw Mill Colliery, a bastion of the Union of Democratic Mineworkers, was just as corrosive. 'Not long after the strike a bloke from Daw Mill came here to see someone in the canteen and everybody walked out.' Graham, who was out for ten of the twelve months, shakes his head at the memory. 'I went back because I could see that it was a waste of time,' he adds sadly.

He'd only gone down the pit in the first place because that's what his mates did. 'Whether they came from the council houses, like me, or the colliery houses, we all went to the same school and played in the same woods and fields. They were all going to work in the same place and I wanted to be one of them. My dad wasn't very happy. He worked at the Dunlop [factory] and he couldn't understand why I wanted to do a more dirty and dangerous job for less money. Mum had to sign my forms.'

That was in 1972 when he was fifteen. He would be almost thirty-five when the colliery closed. 'I've never really settled anywhere else,' he shrugs. 'I've been a hospital porter, worked in factories, and now I'm doing general maintenance at a company in Rugby. But I've never earned good money and I've never worked with such a great bunch of blokes again. Yes, we had arguments

sometimes but we'd come out and say things face to face rather than going behind each other's backs.'

By now we're strolling around Graham's old stamping ground. The roads of Keresley village are quite steep by Coventry standards and, through gaps in the houses, we can see open countryside. There's now a country park, indeed, where children are playing on an adventure playground.

Then we turn a corner and see that the estate's only pub, the Golden Eagle, is boarded up. Some tattered bunting flutters from an upstairs window as though commemorating happier times. As I recall, there used to be a lively Sunday night 'free and easy' in the back room. Miners with powerful singing voices would hog the limelight for a while, some of them well aware that come six o'clock on Monday morning they'd be plunging into darkness once more.

Graham moved from Keresley to Bedworth when he married in 1980. 'Bedduth', as it's better known round here, was very much a colliery town – as indeed was neighbouring Nuneaton where there's still a flat-topped spoil tip that looks like an extinct volcano and is known as Mount Judd. One Mary Ann Evans, better known in later life as George Eliot, grew up nearby on the Arbury estate. It was owned by the Newdigate family, sinkers of many a shaft, including Newdigate Colliery some five miles from Keresley yet connected underground.

'I walked it once,' Graham says proudly. 'Went down the shaft at Keresley and came up at Newdigate.' And as soon as he came out into the open air, he'd reach for his cigarettes as so many miners did. He used to stave off the craving for nicotine underground by taking snuff. 'I must have picked it up from the old blokes I used to work with,' he says. 'Anyway, there was a brand called Kenglow and that became my nickname. Everybody had another name down the pit.'

Mog Stevenson was known as 'fives and threes'. Well, he had five fingers on one hand and three on the other and dominoes was a popular game in the club and the Golden Eagle. If that sounds cruel then Mog certainly wouldn't take offence. 'Not a bit of it,' he chuckles down the phone from his current home in Hythe, Kent. 'That's just the way it was with the lads down the pit. We still enjoy a bit of banter, but these days we have to do it on Facebook.'

So was the loss of those fingers just another mining accident?

'No, I did it when I was a kid.'

But Mog was underground on the evening of Friday, 10 December 1982, when an explosion injured twenty-six Keresley men, seven of them seriously. 'By that time I was a deputy and we'd been doing some routine safety checks when it happened,' he recalls. 'It blew me about fifteen or twenty yards and I got a bang on my foot.' That didn't stop him trying to help dig out others who had been half-buried alive. 'You couldn't see or breathe for a while, but eventually the air cleared a bit,' he adds in a matter-of-fact sort of way.

Having worked at pits in Accrington and Burnley, Mog had come down to Coventry in 1968 on a coach full of Lancashire miners. 'I was the only one to stay,' he says. 'I had a wife and young kids at the time and it seemed like a good opportunity.' (He's now on his fourth wife and the youngest of his seven children is ten. Mog is sixty-six.)

Like many an incomer from the North, it took him time to adjust to seams soaring above his head. 'At Keresley they were up to fifteen feet high in places. We'd been used to crawling around in under three feet. I brought my kneepads with me and for a while I couldn't get out of the habit of kneeling down at the face. In Lancashire we'd been used to working with picks and shovels. This was the first time I'd used long-wall shearers to cut coal.'

By 1991 he was an over-man at Coventry and he stayed on site to close down a colliery he had come to love. Then the tribe of Mog carried on moving south and finished up on the Kent coast. 'I was offered a job on the Channel Tunnel and eventually became technical manager with Eurotunnel.' As crew leader, he was expected to be able to drive a train and, yes, he had to train for it. 'At one point I remember taking over the controls while we were going at 240 kilometres per hour from Paris to Bordeaux.'

Driving a train used to be every schoolboy's dream. Going down the pit sounds like a nightmare to most of us. Not Mog, though. 'I never wanted it to close,' he reflects. 'Whichever pit you worked at it was always the same. You may not have liked everyone on the workforce, but you got on when you were underground because you had to.'

Like many a former miner, I suspect, he has lost that special feeling of being a breed apart from other men. No wonder Keresley always seemed like a place apart from the rest of Coventry.

Right: Coventry Colliery, one of the most advanced in the country.

Left: The monument to the men who worked at the pit at Prologis Business Park.

SNOWDOWN, BETTESHANGER AND TILMANSTONE

THE GARDEN OF ENGLAND is not green today. It's white. An unexpected blizzard has disrupted rail services in the Southeast even more than usual. At least there's plenty of time to contemplate the sheer unlikelihood of coal mining in Kent. Betteshanger Colliery, sited close to Deal, that quaint seaside town with its two castles, its pier and well-preserved Georgian architecture, was shut down in 1989. Chislet, which closed twenty years previously, was closer to Whitstable with its oyster festival, its beach huts, its thriving restaurants and galleries.

Today I'm on my way – eventually – to the site of Snowdown Colliery, so the snow seems ironically appropriate. Why 'ironically'? Because there was nothing cold about the lower depths of Snowdown in its heyday. In parts it went down to almost 3,000 feet below the lush and fecund fields of Kent and was known to the men who worked there as The Inferno.

They would strip down to their underpants or, in some cases, work stark naked apart from their kneepads, belts and boots – boots that had to be emptied of sweat at regular intervals. Nearby Betteshanger wasn't quite so deep or quite so hot. It was warm and muggy enough, mind you, for miners to shed their clothes with equal abandon. 'Underpants were a bit baggy in the days when I started there,' says Jim Davies, now seventy. 'So we used to work in women's briefs to keep the old tackle away from catching on anything. The bloke I was having a drink with last night was about twenty stone and his dad was even bigger, but he used to send me down to Marks and Spencer's to buy his knickers for him.'

Cue knowing grins and chuckles around the table at the Heritage Centre in Aylesham, the village built in the 1920s to house Snowdown miners. Ladies' underwear, it seems, was not unknown at The Inferno. Men there were equally wary of putting the old tackle at risk. Apart from anything else, the oppressive heat attracted insects such as crickets and even the occasional swarm of hornets. 'I was stung once,' Colin Owen recalls with a shudder. Not on your . . .? 'No, on my hip,' he adds hurriedly. 'We had to take salt tablets as well as carry what we called a "Dudley" with eight pints of water apiece.'

Colin is here with his brother Keith. Both were face-workers and, like the other old miners gathered among the monochrome memorabilia of their former life in another century, both are well muffled on this chilly morning as we discuss the hellish heat of their former workplace.

You don't have to be a genealogist to realise that Davies and Owen are Welsh names. Men from the valleys moved here in some numbers during the inter-war depression. Some walked all the way, lacking the price of the train fare. Jim's father came in 1931 on the promise of a job, a house and a place at fly-half in the burgeoning Betteshanger rugby club. He had come from a colliery in the Rhondda just down the road from where Colin and Keith's old man had worked. There was a strong Welsh presence, too, at Kent's other collieries – particularly at Chislet. Tilmanstone, meanwhile, had more than its fair share of Somerset men.

In fact, colliers came to East Kent from all over the UK in the first half of the last century. Snowdown was not only an inferno; it was also a Tower of Babel. The jabber of many accents and dialects could be heard in the cramped confines of the cage as it plunged down the shaft into the bowels of the earth. 'In our road there used to be Geordies, Scots and Yorkshire people as well as Welsh,' Keith remembers. Like his brother and Jim, he talks like a man of Kent. When it comes to international rugby, however, their hearts belong to the Millennium Stadium, Cardiff, rather than much-closer Twickenham.

Why the influx of miners from elsewhere? Because Kent had no mining tradition when coal was first found there and the coal owners needed men who knew what they were doing.

And what did the incomers find when they arrived? They were met with widespread discrimination from the indigenous population. Signs reminiscent of those that greeted the first West Indian immigrants to the UK would go up in the front windows of boarding houses and flats-to-let in Deal, Dover and Ramsgate. 'No dogs or miners,' read the stark message. Shops would advertise 'Miners' bacon' when they wanted to get rid of the scraggiest piece of gristle. A local newspaper carried the headline: 'Man in fight with miner'.

Memories were long in the towns, villages and seaside resorts here in the far Southeast. Stories were still rife about the wild behaviour of the 'sinkers', the hard-drinking, frequently brawling men who came to sink the shafts when coal had first been discovered. Twenty-two of them had been drowned at Snowdown after the first shaft hit water at 260 feet. But on 19 November 1912, five years after the first sod had been turned, coal was finally brought to the surface.

By that time, the Shakespeare Colliery at Dover had already been abandoned as a bad job. Digging around the white-cliffed gateway to this island built on coal had only

begun after the first Channel Tunnel project had also been abandoned some time in the 1890s. Nigh-on a century would pass before the tunnel finally came to fruition. Some technical staff from the three remaining mines that had closed in the second half of the 1980s found work on its construction. Few miners were employed, however, despite what you might imagine would be impeccable credentials for burrowing under the sea.

Kent miners had a reputation for militancy. Had not would-be pickets been turned back by police at the Dartford Tunnel during the bitter dispute of 1984–5? Had they not prevented the movement of fuel into the power stations of London and the Southeast during the strike of 1972? Had their fathers and grandfathers not included a fair sprinkling of men who had been locked out of other collieries after the National Strike of 1926?

The answer to all those questions is yes, which helps to explain why the recruitment policy of the company building the tunnel could well have been influenced by the so-called 'silent McCarthyists' of the Economic League. Founded in 1919, the League was evidently still targeting what it saw as left-wing activists seventy years later when Betteshanger closed and poor old Jim found himself on one of its blacklists.

He wasn't even a member of the National Union of Mineworkers, having long since joined NACODs (the National Association of Colliery Overmen, Deputies and Shotfirers). The former face-worker had moved into management. Indeed, he had been in charge of underground operations at Betteshanger and is widely referred to round here as 'the last miner in Kent', having overseen the filling-in of the shafts and then the locking of the gates. 'I remember going home on that last day and thinking to myself, "Christ, that's the end of it after thirty-three years of my working life".'

Still, he had another job to go to. Or so he thought. 'Two days before I was due to start, I received a letter telling me not to come. Eventually an ex-Snowdown man told me about the League's blacklist. As it happens, one of my names is Idwell and a bloke called Idwell Davies had been put away during the strike. They'd simply got his identity and mine mixed up. So I rang up the Channel Tunnel Company and the bloke on the end of the line got very agitated and assured me that "we don't operate that kind of system". But within two hours of me pointing out the case of mistaken identity, one of my former colleagues knocked on the door and told me, "There's a job for you at the Tunnel."'

He never took it. The blacklist saga had taken a while to unfold and, in the meantime, Jim had set up his own trophy shop. Eventually he would supply international

Below, right: Snowdown miners showing off their musical skills.

Above: Supplies of water were desperately needed for The Inferno workers.

companies with engraved glassware but, for the time being, he had a thriving market closer to home. Having felt rejected by the rest of the county, Kent miners had turned in on themselves and built up strong sporting and cultural competitions within and between their respective pit villages. Every colliery had its own brass band and male voice choir, pigeon club, fishing club, bowls, rugby, cricket and football club. And more. Most have survived to this day and kept the 'Colliery' part of the title. What they haven't kept, for obvious reasons, is the miner element of the membership. The 'last miner in Kent' closed the gates of the last colliery for the last time a quarter of a century ago.

Jim now gives talks on the area's mining heritage to organisations such as the Folkestone History Society and finds himself booked up for almost a year ahead. 'Last night it was the Kent Vintage Tractor Association,' he confides. 'They were really interested. Questions went on for an hour.'

Below: The statue to a Kent miner at the entrance of Fowlmead Country Park.

Right: Betteshanger wasn't quite as hot as The Inferno of Snowdown, but was quite hot enough.

A century after those incoming pioneers of Kentish mining received such a frosty welcome from the indigenous population, it would seem everybody wants to know about them. It was rather different when the pits were still open, Jim recalls. 'We played rugby all over the county, representing Snowdown, Tilmanstone or Betteshanger Collieries, and our hosts would say, "Oh, are you from up North then?" You might be in Tunbridge Wells, for instance, and people would be completely unaware that there were any pits in the county.'

In a moment Jim's going to take me for a drive round to see what's left. But first Keith gives me a short tour of the display boards in the heritage centre. Near a 1971 newspaper headline proclaiming 'Kent Coal Queen is Aylesham mother of two' is a photograph of the Snowdown Colliery Welfare Male Voice Choir taken in 1948. Every one a miner and every one wearing a white shirt tucked into trousers belted with a sash – apart from the guest contralto soloist, that is, also known as Keith and Colin's mum. 'Madam Owen', as she was called after a trip to France, was still with the choir when they won a trophy at the Eisteddfod in 1955. Those links with Wales were never severed.

There was also a more obscure link with the English Midlands. Three former Snowdown Colliery Welfare FC players found themselves on the books at Coventry City. Among them was that formidable former miner George Curtis, who captained Jimmy Hill's side when they were promoted to the top flight in 1967 and was co-manager with John Sillett when the Sky Blues won the FA Cup twenty years later. Keith went to school with him. 'Bit of a brute on the field was George,' he recalls, almost wincing at the memory. 'But he never forgot where he came from. He brought the Cup down here in a holdall in 1987 and we all had a drink out of it.'

By that time Snowdown Collliery had already closed. So had Tilmanstone. Betteshanger would hang on for another two years. As in so many parts of the country, the villages built to house their employees had lost their focus, the very reason for their existence. Aylesham has also lost its secondary school, the children bussed elsewhere. And when they're bussed back again for the final time, what do they find at the end of their school days, those who don't go on to higher education?

'There is a problem with sixteen to twenty-four-year-olds,' says Jason Rose of the Aylesham Skills Factory,

which is doing its best to address the issue. 'We've just trained up fourteen lads for trackside work on the railway,' he adds.

In the village there's a Co-op, a health centre, a working men's club and what is now known as the Aylesham Welfare Leisure Centre. No pub. And the site of the former Snowdown pit? Well, the winding house and the fitting shop are still there behind barbed wire and rusting gates held together by a large and shiny padlock.

As we drive on down the road, rural Kent reasserts itself. A thatched cottage here, a rustic-looking inn there, a cricket field nearby. It's difficult to believe now that miners co-existed with this comparatively comfortable world.

Elvington was another twentieth-century pit village, built to house the colliers of Tilmanstone. Most mornings they'd stride or stroll across the fields to work. The brickworks that once stood on the colliery site appears to have closed down. Tilmanstone (formerly Kent) Salads are still there, though. A few miners found work by moving from coal to coleslaw production. On the site of the colliery yard, meanwhile, is a caravan park at the centre of which is a diner with a lit-up sign inviting us to 'Eat at Tom's'.

We don't. Instead we move on to The Circle, where some of the Betteshanger miners lived, clustered around the pit in curved rows. 'There used to be a shop there called Jones's,' says Jim, pointing to what is now a private house. 'The miners used to go in for tea and a fag at the end of the shift, leaving all their Dudleys hanging on the fence.' If the end of the shift happened to coincide with licensed opening times, they might go for a pint instead to what is now the Betteshanger Social Club, run by volunteers and sited next door to an enormous electricity sub-station.

The offices where Jim worked when he reached management level are now occupied by a private company. Almond House is named after Geoff Almond, the last miner to be killed at Betteshanger. He was crushed to death only a month or two before the closure. 'Hell of a good cricketer he was,' says Jim, shaking his head.

Do you miss this place?

'Christ, yes.'

We drive on to Fowlmead Country Park where first the colliery railway and later lorries used to dump rock and spoil that had been separated from the coal. The park now hosts the Kent Miners' Festival, an event that attracts up to 12,000 people every August. At the gateway to the park is a statue to a Kent miner, squatting and naked (mercifully) only from the waist up. And, before you ask, he's wearing trousers rather than knickers. On the plinth beneath him is a list of 'those who lost their lives during the life of the Kent coalfield'. Jim collated the names and assures me that there are well over 200 of them.

He still lives at Mill Hill, the estate on the edge of Deal that accommodated those Betteshanger miners who didn't live at The Circle. In fact he and his wife Jean have bought the house where he lived as a child. 'Her parents came from Yorkshire, but we were born within fifty yards of each other,' he says. Tight-knit yet disparate: that was the nature of the communities that grew up around the Kent mines.

Mill Hill feels very different from the rest of Deal. Just past its borders are flint walls, clapperboard houses, an ancient church and prosperous-looking shops. And then there's the station.

On the interminable train journey back to Charing Cross, I dip back into Malcolm Pitt's book on the Kent miners and the 1972 miners' strike. It's called *The World on Our Backs*, a title that tells you everything you need to know about how those men and their families felt about their isolation from the rest of Kent and indeed the rest of

Face to face with the face at Betteshanger.

the British coalfield. Pitt was a ripper at Tilmanstone and a member of the Communist Party of Great Britain who, like Graham Greene, somehow managed to bridge the yawning chasm between communism and Catholicism. After the mines closed, he worked for the Catholic Bishops' Conference of England and Wales and met Pope John Paul II on several occasions.

His book was published in 1978 when the three local pits were still in full production. On page twenty-four he writes:

Going to work on the bus through the Kent countryside for an afternoon shift is a sheer test of will. The bus passes through orchards and fields, past country pubs still serving dinnertime drinkers. Someone is bound to express the forlorn hope that the bus will break down, or get wedged between two parked cars or, as they pass the Eastry Mental Hospital, voice the opinion that the only mad people in the world are the men in the pits. The ordeal continues until the men are in the cage and down the pit. A team of men will move off from the canteen when someone summons up the will to say, 'Come on, let's get in there and get it over with'. It is said with the finality of a prison sentence. Miners often say that the worst part of a shift is getting into the pit.

Mind you, it must have been easier on days like this, I reflect, looking out over the snowy wastes of the Garden of England. At least you knew that you were going to get warm. Rather too warm in The Inferno at the bottom of Snowdown.

BIBLIOGRAPHY

Armstrong, Stephen. *The Road to Wigan Pier Revisited*, Constable, 2011

Brooks, Tony, and Watton, John. *King Edward Mine*, Cornish Hillside Publications, 2002

Brooks, Tony. *Devon's Last Metal Mine*, Cornish Hillside Publications, 2004

Florence Mine Heritage Centre. *The Last Deep Working Iron Ore Mine in Europe*, Kent Valley Colour Printers, Kendal

Goodyear, Simon. *The Gerry Hitchens Story: From Mine to Milan*, Breedon Books Publishing, 2009

Harvey, Dave. *Where We Belong*, The Whitehouse Press

Minchinton, Walter. *A Guide to Industrial Archaeology Sites in Britain*, Granada Publishing, 1984

Orwell, George. *The Road to Wigan Pier*, Penguin Modern Classics, 1937

Pearson, Harry. *Slipless in Settle*, Little Brown, 2010

Pitt, Malcolm. *The World on Our Backs: The Kent Miners and the 1972 Miners' Strike*, Lawrence and Wishart, 1979

Skelly, John W. *Poems of the Pits Volume Two*, Printexpress (Cumbria) Ltd

Tuck, James. *The Collieries of Northumberland Volume One*, Trade Union Printing Services

Williams H.V. *Cornwall's Old Mines*, Top Mark Press

PICTURE CREDITS

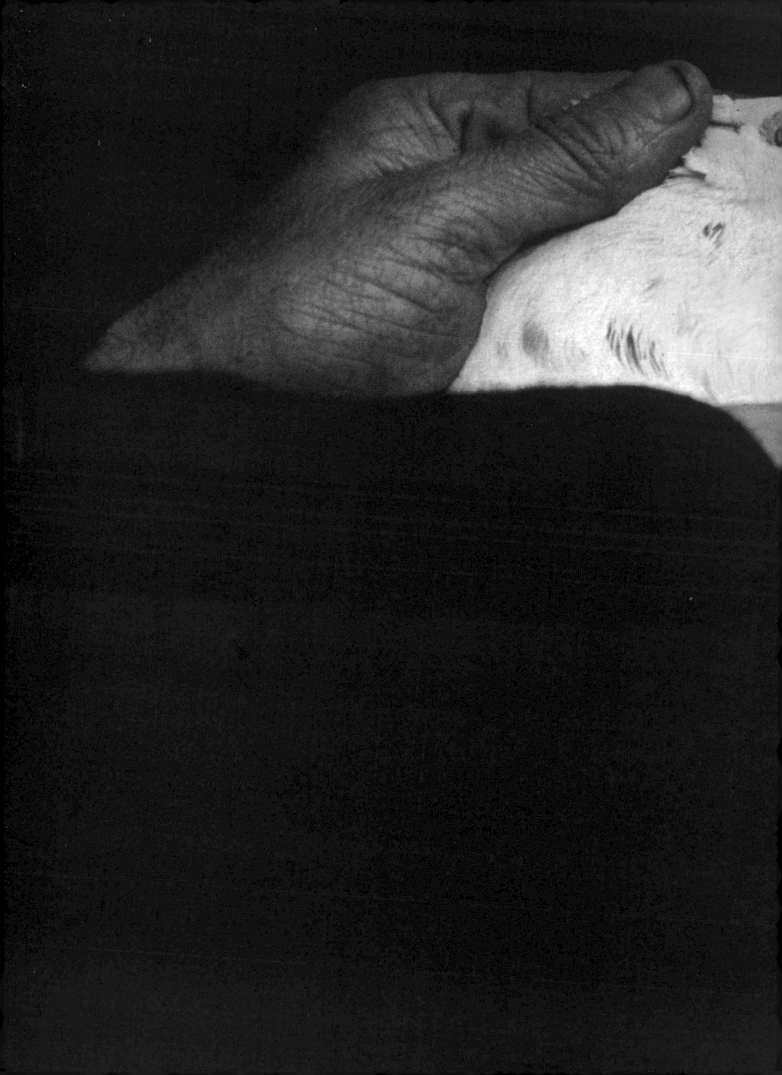